AS LONG AS THEY'RE HAPPY

A Farcical Comedy in Three Acts

by

VERNON SYLVAINE

SAMUEL FRENCH

LONDON

NEW YORK   TORONTO   SYDNEY   HOLLYWOOD

ISBN 0 573 01026 9

Please note our NEW ADDRESS:

Samuel French Ltd
52 Fitzroy Street London W1P 6JR
Tel: 01 - 387 9373

AS LONG AS THEY'RE HAPPY

Presented by Linnit and Dunfee Ltd at the Garrick Theatre, London, on 8th July 1953 with the following cast of characters:

(in the order of their appearance)

GWENDOLINE	Susan Lyall-Grant
LINDA	Virginia Hewett
PATRICIA	Sally Cooper
STELLA BENTLEY	Dorothy Dickson
JOHN BENTLEY	Jack Buchanan
BOBBY DENVER	David Hutcheson
HERMANN SCHNEIDER	Frederick Berger
MICHAEL KENLEY	Stephen Hancock
PETER PEMBER	Nigel Green
PEARL	Madi Hedd
CORINNE	Jean Burgess
BARNABY	John Boyd-Brent

The play directed by ROY RICH
The setting designed by FANNY TAYLOR

SYNOPSIS OF SCENES

The action of the play passes in the lounge of John Bentley's house near Regent's Park, London

ACT I
Morning

ACT II
SCENE 1   The same. Afternoon
SCENE 2   The same. Evening

ACT III
SCENE 1   The same. Night
SCENE 2   The same. Next morning

Time—the present

ACKNOWLEDGEMENTS

WE are indebted to Messrs Keith Prowse & Co. Ltd for permission to reprint lines from the song *Sweet and Lovely*, and to Messrs Campbell, Connelly & Co. Ltd for permission to reprint the words of the song *Please Don't Forget to Remember*.

IMPORTANT

PERMISSION to perform the play does not include permission to use the songs mentioned in the text.

Where the theatre or hall in which the play is being performed is licensed by the Performing Right Society a return must be made in the usual way; but where the theatre or hall is not so licensed permission must be sought in respect of each song from the respective publishers of the music.

A list of the songs used in the play will be found on page 79.

Photograph by Denis de Marney

AS LONG AS THEY'RE HAPPY

ACT I

SCENE—*The lounge of John Bentley's house, near Regent's Park. Morning.*

There are french windows at R leading to the garden. The main entrance to the lounge is through an arch at RC. At LC there is an arched or squared recess in which can be seen the stairs with decorative wrought-iron banisters, leading to upstairs. Down L there is a door leading to a dining-room off stage. There is a chair and table below the french windows. At R of the entrance arch and facing the audience is a radiogram. Through the arch can be seen a long table against the wall, and electric fittings on the wall. There is a small window in the off-stage R wall. On stage, L of the arch and facing the audience, is a long narrow table carrying bottles of cocktails and spirits, a vase with flowers, books and telephone. Against the L wall is a medium grand piano, with a piano stool up stage facing the audience. At RC there is a settee with a narrow sofa table behind and against it. At LC there is a low upholstered armchair. Above the door down L is a chair. There are the usual light fittings and suitable carpet, rugs, pictures and etceteras. Where architecturally possible the set breaks at slight angles.

(See the Ground Plan and Photograph of the scene)

When the CURTAIN *rises, it is about 11 a.m. on a spring morning. The sun shines through from the garden. A moment—and* GWENDOLINE *cautiously descends the stairs LC. She is an attractive girl of sixteen, slim, slight and sensitive. She wears pyjamas, slippers and dressing-gown, and her hair is attractively dressed. She glances about the lounge, then moves quickly to the phone up stage. She lifts the receiver and dials a number.*

GWEN. Hullo. Is that the Savoy Hotel? . . . This is Mr J. Arthur Rank's secretary speaking. Would you put me through to Mr Robert Denver, please? . . . Mr Robert Denver . . . Well, perhaps you know him as Bobby Denver . . . Thank you. (*She rests the receiver on the table, hurries to the archway, looks off stage, then hurries back to the phone*) Hullo? . . . He's what? . . . In his bath? . . . Well, can't he get *out* of his bath? . . . Oh, but listen, this is very urgent. Mr J. Arthur Rank is waiting right here to speak to him . . . Would you do that, please? . . . The number is Hampstead four-three-two-seven. . . . Yes, as soon as possible . . . Thank you. Good-bye.

(GWEN *smilingly replaces the receiver as* LINDA *enters through the archway.* LINDA, *maid to the Bentley household, is about thirty. She*

1

is a thin, worried type, but she doesn't drop her aitches and she is not a caricature. She wears a little white apron in front of her black skirt)

What do you want, Linda?

LINDA. Well, Harry's called for Mr Skeffington, miss, and I can't find him anywhere.

GWEN (*moving to the settee*) He's in my bedroom.

LINDA. He hasn't been there all night, has he?

GWEN. He certainly has. I felt lonely.

LINDA. Well, for heaven's sake don't let your father know. He's beginning to proper hate Mr Skeffington.

GWEN (*sitting on the settee*) Poor Daddy. I feel so sorry for him.

LINDA. Why?

GWEN. He's getting old and crotchety.

LINDA. Nonsense! Your father's in the full flush of ripe middle age.

GWEN (*wistfully*) Whenever I think of him now I see the leaves falling—and the corn bending.

LINDA. Yes—you let him hear you talking like that and you'll be doing some bending.

GWEN (*smiling*) Oh, no. I'm not a child any longer. I'm sixteen. I'm a woman! Ready to fulfil my destiny.

LINDA (*moving to the stairs*) I don't like that sort of talk. I'll get Mr Skeffington.

(LINDA *exits up the stairs. The phone rings.* GWEN *rises and excitedly hurries to lift the receiver)*

GWEN. Hullo? . . . Yes, that's right. Oh, thank you. I'll put him through to Mr Rank. (*She taps the receiver rest to simulate an exchange plug noise*) Hullo? Is that Mr Robert Denver? . . . (*She gives a deep sigh*) Oh, Bobby! I love you! I adore you! It's Gwendoline. Hullo . . . Hullo . . . Hullo . . .

(GWEN *smilingly replaces the receiver as* LINDA *descends the stairs with Mr Skeffington)*

(*Taking the dog's lead*) All right, Linda—I'll take him.

LINDA. He can't stay in here.

GWEN. Why not?

LINDA. He's so dirty.

GWEN. I like him like that.

LINDA. Miss Gwen, I don't know what's come over you lately. I think you're sickening for something.

(LINDA *exits through the archway)*

GWEN (*picking up the dog*) Skeffy! He spoke to me! (*Enraptured*) Right close to my ear, I heard his voice. He said, "Who the hell are you?" And when I told him he slammed down the receiver. He didn't just replace it. (*Enraptured*) He slammed it down!

(*The phone rings.* GWEN *hurries to it and lifts the receiver*)

(*Hopefully*) Hullo? (*Irritably*) No. How *could* it be Euston Station?

(GWEN *bangs the receiver down as* LINDA *hurries in through the archway*)

LINDA (*excitedly*) Miss Gwen—your sister's here!

GWEN (*surprised*) Which one?

LINDA. Miss Patricia—I mean Mrs Pember.

(PATRICIA *enters briskly through the archway. She carries a small Paris Airline valise. She is twenty-one, brisk, forthright, modern and hardboiled. She is wearing very tight trousers, exaggerated brogues of light yellow, red socks, a yellow jersey with a plain rounded neck, a dull green jacket, and a necklet of outsize imitation pearls to match her ear-rings. Her hair is brushed back flat and tight and a red ribbon holds the horse's tail effect at the back of her head. She has just the suspicion of a black eye*)

PAT. One hour to fly over from Paris, and three to get through the damn customs. Hullo, Gwen.

GWEN (*moving* C) Pat! I scarcely recognized you.

PAT. I haven't been away all that long, have I?

GWEN. No, of course not. Are you all right?

PAT (*as she throws her small valise on to the settee table*) I'm fine. Where's Mother?

GWEN. Out. You've got a black eye.

PAT. Yes. I bumped into somebody.

GWEN. Is Peter with you?

PAT. No. I left him in Paris.

GWEN. But what about your honeymoon?

PAT. I left that in Paris too.

GWEN. Is anything wrong?

PAT (*taking a packet of French cigarettes from her hip pocket*) For God's sake! What *is* all this? I've just flown over to buy some clothes, that's all.

(PAT *extracts a cigarette and replaces the packet as* LINDA *takes Mr Skeffington from Gwen*)

LINDA (*as she does so*) She doesn't look happy, Miss Gwen. I can always tell unhappiness. I remember when my mother married my father, I could see at once she wasn't happy.

PAT (*having lit the cigarette*) Linda . . .

LINDA. Yes, miss?

PAT. Get to hell out of it.

LINDA. Yes, miss.

PAT. And bring me a sandwich.

LINDA. Yes, miss—er—Mrs—madam.

(LINDA *exits confusedly through the archway with Mr Skeffington*)

PAT (*moving to sit on the settee; briskly*) Have you heard from Corinne?

GWEN (*moving to the* L *end of the settee*) Not since she went to New York.

PAT. It was quite funny, really—two of us suddenly getting married.

GWEN. I couldn't see anything funny about it. Marriage is a sacred undertaking.

PAT (*smiling*) Oh, dear. Still taking life seriously? Are you going to bed or getting up?

GWEN. I'm convalescing. Daddy thinks I've been ill.

PAT. Oh? What's the matter?

GWEN (*turning and moving to* LC) I just happen to have lost my appetite, that's all.

PAT. In love with somebody?

GWEN. Of course not.

PAT. Does Father know?

GWEN. Nobody knows.

PAT. Well, take it slowly, Gwen. Don't rush into anything.

GWEN (*turning to look at Pat*) Oh, Pat, what's wrong?

PAT (*irritably*) Nothing, nothing! I'm just tired, that's all.

GWEN. Why are you dressed like a morbid fisherman?

(PAT *rises and moves up stage to pour herself a neat whisky*)

PAT. My husband *likes* me to dress like a morbid fisherman. Peter is an Existentialist. Our flat is in the Boulevard St Germain. And, in the Boulevard St Germain, all Existentialists dress like morbid fishermen.

GWEN. How did you get that black eye?

PAT (*turning*) An elderly French aristocrat tried to crack Peter with a bottle. He missed him and hit me. (*She drinks some of her whisky*)

GWEN. What dreadful sort of life are you leading in Paris?

PAT (*moving down to the* R *end of the settee*) There are no words to describe it. It's the far end of hell. If ever I have any children they'll be certified at birth. (*She drinks some more whisky*)

GWEN. What on earth will Father say?

(PAT *bangs her glass down on to the settee table*)

PAT. Gwen, I've been living where policemen walk about in fours. Our flat is a converted cellar with an outside inconvenience, and our landlady is one of the original knitters under the original guillotine. To me the word " father " sounds about as frightening as the word "pussy cat".

(PAT *stumps out her cigarette into an ashtray at the* R *end of the settee table, as* LINDA *hurries in through the archway carrying a sandwich on a plate*)

LINDA (*moving down to Pat*) I'm afraid this is the best I can do, Miss Patricia. Oh, dear. I can't get used to your marriage.

PAT (*taking the plate*) Nor can I. (*She lifts the top bread of the sandwich*) What in hell's name is this?

LINDA. I think it's liver sausage, miss. It was all right when I had it for breakfast.

(PAT *places the plate and sandwich on the settee table as* STELLA BENTLEY *is heard calling, off stage*)

STELLA (*off*) Linda!

LINDA (*to Pat*) There's Mrs Bentley! I reckon she'll just about fall down when she sees *you*.

(LINDA *hurries away through the archway as* PAT *moves down* R)

PAT. Oh, hell!

GWEN (*moving* C) What's the matter?

PAT. I forgot I'd have to go through all this.

GWEN. How do you mean?

PAT. Darling, you know Stella. She's the most wonderful step-mother anybody could have, but—oh gosh!—that exuberance! Any moment now—and she'll simply burst into the room—probably with a loud cry of "Pat, darling! This is the most wonderful moment of my life!" I sometimes wish she'd never left the stage. She'd be a dame or something by now.

GWEN. How you've changed.

PAT. So have you. You're walking on air—and you look quite beautiful. How long have you known him?

GWEN (*moving away* L) Be quiet!

STELLA (*off*) Pat, darling! This is the most wonderful moment of my life!

(PAT *laughs—and* STELLA *arrives in the archway. She* **is** *a most attractive woman—young for her thirty-nine years—and faultlessly dressed for spring out-of-doors in town. She carries a large bunch of yellow roses. She remains framed in the archway as she smilingly glances round the room. Her eyes rest on Pat, then she looks at Gwen as she moves forward*)

(*To* Gwen) Where is she?

(GWEN *silently indicates her sister.* STELLA *moves down* C *as she stares at Pat*)

Oh, no! I thought you were somebody from the Chinese laundry.

PAT (*moving to* RC *below the settee*) Stella, please don't be face-tious. I'm tired.

STELLA (*over-sympathetic*) Of course you are. (*She moves to Pat*) You poor darling. I've never seen anybody look so tired. (*Quietly*) You can tell me about the black eye when we're alone together. (*Brightly*) How's Peter and how's Paris—and above all—are you happy? (*Without waiting for an answer*) Darling, those trousers! Are they meant to be as tight as that?

GWEN. Mother, for heaven's sake!

STELLA. And those brogues! Of course, they'll last for ever. I simply can't wait to see what Peter's wearing. Where is he?

PAT. In prison.

STELLA. Splendid. (*After a sudden reaction*) What did you say?

PAT (*making unemotional statements*) Peter is in a small prison, just off the Rue Bergère. He's been charged with assaulting a gendarme and smashing up the *Petit Poisson* Night Club. I've flown over here to borrow five hundred thousand francs from Father.

STELLA. *What?*

GWEN (*to Pat*) You're fooling.

PAT (*sitting c of the settee*) I'm not.

STELLA. But what happened?

PAT (*taking the plate from the table behind her*) We were celebrating my birthday. The party got a little wild and Peter had too much to drink. For an Englishman he's very excitable.

STELLA (*sitting L of Pat*) Does he *always* hit you in the eye when he's excited?

PAT. He's *never* hit me. Somebody else did that, quite accidentally. (*She takes a bite of the sandwich*)

GWEN (*moving LC*) It was a French aristocrat, and he hit her with a bottle.

STELLA (*to Pat*) Well, thank heaven you're meeting some nice people. How much is five hundred thousand francs?

PAT. About five hundred pounds.

STELLA. Is Peter in a cell?

PAT. He was last night. He's probably on his way to Devil's Island by now.

STELLA. Hasn't he got his passport with him?

PAT. What's that got to do with it?

STELLA. It definitely states that he's got to be looked after and afforded every protection. Anyway, I thought the French were our allies or something. This is dreadful! It'll kill your poor father.

(PAT *has another bite at the sandwich*)

GWEN. Oh, Mother, don't be melodramatic.

STELLA (*turning*) Gwen, how dare you talk to me like that? When I'm so upset, too. Go back to bed at once!

GWEN. Why should I? There's nothing the matter with me.

STELLA. I'm not thinking of you. I want to talk to Pat.

GWEN. So do I.

STELLA. Well, you can speak to her later. She's just come straight from Paris, and quite obviously she has something to tell me that a girl of your age shouldn't hear.

GWEN (*moving to the stairs*) You're getting more like Father every day.

STELLA. How do you mean?

GWEN (*as she ascends the stairs*) Whenever he mentions Paris—he winks.

(GWEN *exits up the stairs*)

STELLA (*excitedly*) Pat! I can't wait to hear about you and Peter. The marriage *was* quite legal, wasn't it?

PAT (*throwing the plate and sandwich on to the settee*) Good God, of course it was!

STELLA. Is Peter still writing plays?

PAT. Yes—he wrote one last Thursday.

STELLA (*rising and moving to* C) But that's wonderful! *You* can continue your acting and he can write the loveliest parts for you.

PAT. No, Stella. You don't understand. He doesn't write plays that can be acted.

STELLA (*wistfully*) Oh, how that takes me back!

PAT. To him the theatre is a servile medium through which he expresses his views as an Existentialist.

STELLA (*completely lost*) Ah, yes, of course, dear . . .

PAT. He's fifty years ahead of his time.

STELLA (*happily*) Well, you must just try and keep up with him.

PAT. He doesn't lead the life of an ordinary individual. He's quite strange—really very queer.

STELLA. Darling, you don't mean in any way your father wouldn't understand?

PAT. Most emphatically no! (*Wildly*) But I can't go on living with him!

STELLA. Why not? You love him, don't you?

PAT. Yes, I love him, but I don't like him. He's as crazy as a coot!

STELLA. Darling, all playwrights are.

PAT. But he's not content with writing plays! A fortnight ago he decided to take up sculpture. Our only wardrobe is full of clay, and our bedroom is full of pornographic statues. He sleeps all day and gets up at midnight. He's growing a beard and he eats his food with his fingers. He wears pale blue shorts and rides a red bicycle. He drinks like a fish and gives the victory sign in reverse to all policemen.

STELLA (*moving to the piano*) Oh, Pat! You don't know how I envy you.

PAT (*amazed*) What?

(STELLA *places the roses on the piano, and turns*)

STELLA. For fourteen years I've been married to a man whose motto is "Steady as she goes". For fourteen years I've listened to nothing but talk about stocks and shares and bulls and bears. I've survived it because I transferred my own ambitions to Corinne, you, and Gwen. But believe me, Pat, after the dull and ordered security of life with your father, Peter's temperament would lift me to the skies. I sometimes feel I'd like to set fire to this house, seduce the vicar, and go busking in the West End.

(LINDA *hurries in through the archway*)

LINDA. Mrs Bentley! The master's come home.

(PAT *rises as* STELLA *gasps*)

STELLA. Oh no! Linda, whatever you do don't tell him Mrs Pember is here.

LINDA (*reluctantly*) Very well, ma'am.

(LINDA *exits as* STELLA *indicates the room* L)

STELLA. Pat, wait in there. I want to do this my way.

PAT (*grabbing her valise*) I've got to get that five hundred pounds.

STELLA. I'll get it for you. I just want to make quite sure that your father's in the right mood to hand it over.

PAT (*crossing* L *below Stella*) Okay.

STELLA. And when you meet him for heaven's sake pretend to be happy.

PAT (*angrily*) I am happy!

(PAT *exits into the room* L *as* STELLA *moves to take up the yellow roses.* JOHN BENTLEY'S *voice is heard*)

JOHN (*off*) And what's this slipper doing here?

LINDA (*off*) That's Mr Skeffington's, sir.

JOHN (*off*) I told you to keep that damn dog out of the house. The place is getting like a bear garden.

LINDA (*off*) Yes, sir.

(JOHN BENTLEY *enters through the archway. Quite obviously he is not in a good mood. About forty-six, well built and fit, good-looking, well-groomed. There is a certain pompousness about him but he has an attractive personality. He is dressed in a short black jacket and carefully creased trousers, etc. He carries the "Financial Times"*)

STELLA (*moving to him*) John, dear. You're home very early, aren't you? (*Holding up the roses*) Look! Aren't they lovely? Is anything wrong? You're not ill, are you? Will you be staying for lunch?

JOHN. Taking your questions in the correct order, the answers are—yes, very, I hope not, and I don't think so.

STELLA. Oh. Well, thank goodness for that. Shall I put them in water for you?

JOHN (*surprised*) Are they for me?

STELLA. Of course.

JOHN. Why—what have I done?

STELLA (*smilingly*) It's the tenth.

JOHN. The tenth?

(JOHN *looks blank.* STELLA *continues*)

STELLA. The tenth of May. The day your first wife left you.

JOHN. Stella, you really are the most tactless person I've ever met!

STELLA. I'm sorry. I thought it was an occasion for rejoicing.

JOHN (*irritably*) Quite possibly it is, in a masochistic sort of way, but we've never remembered it before. Why, for no reason at all, start today?

STELLA. Yes, it was rather silly. I know. I'll pretend *you* gave them to *me*. (*She clasps the roses to her breast and smiles*) There, is that all right?

JOHN. Yes, Stella, that's all right.

(JOHN *has glanced at his wife quite casually and he has not intended to continue looking at her, but he does*)

They look lovelier than ever now. I wish I *had* bought them for you. (*He kisses her on the cheek*)

STELLA (*surprised*) Thank you, John.

JOHN (*moving up stage*) How's Gwen?

STELLA (*moving* L *to put the roses on the piano*) Much better. Quite her old self again.

JOHN (*as he pours himself a whisky*) Good.

STELLA. Not whisky, dear? Not in the morning. You only do that when you're worried.

JOHN (*moving* C *with his glass*) I *am* worried.

STELLA. What's happened? Oh, I did so want you to be in a happy mood. Are those share things going up and down again?

JOHN. No, Stella. It's nothing to do with my work in the City.

STELLA. You mean—it's something important?

(JOHN *reacts, then continues*)

JOHN. This morning, at the office, I received a twenty-five minutes' phone call from Corinne in New York.

STELLA (*anxiously*) She's not ill, is she?

JOHN. No. She sounded quite fighting fit. She sent you her love, and her husband sent his love, and she hoped you were quite well, and her husband hoped you were quite well, and she enquired all about her dog and her canary and her tortoise. She also asked how I was. The rest of the twenty-five minutes was spent explaining why her husband was out of work and impressing upon me the urgent necessity for cabling her a thousand dollars at once.

(STELLA *glances unhappily towards the door* L)

A thousand dollars! How am I supposed to do that? They've only been married two months. (*He drinks some of his whisky*)

STELLA (*feebly*) How much is a thousand dollars in francs?

JOHN. What on earth has that got to do with it?

STELLA. I was just wondering.

JOHN (*moving above the settee table*) She should never have married that damn fellow. She *wouldn't* have done if I'd had *my* way. (*He finishes his whisky*)

STELLA. You're not blaming me for it, are you?

JOHN (*putting his glass on the settee table*) You introduced him to her.

STELLA. And I'm glad I did. Barnaby is masculine and virile. You should have seen him at Olympia.

JOHN. A cowboy, without any cows. A film actor on horseback. A fine husband he'll make.

STELLA. When he's working he earns fabulous money.

JOHN. And whether he's working or not he spends it.

STELLA. Why isn't he working now?

JOHN (*moving* C) Your Bump-along-Barnaby, or whatever he's called, happens to have a carbuncle on his bottom and he can't sit on his horse. That temporary emergency lands Corinne in the bread line.

STELLA. But everyone knows that the film world is chicken one day and feathers the next. It's like the stage.

JOHN (*angrily*) Thank you, I don't want to hear anything about *that* profession! I had Corinne trained to be a private secretary. She could have been safe and secure in an embassy by now.

STELLA. But she didn't want to be a secretary. She wanted to be a veterinary surgeon. I'm quite sure she only married Barnaby because she's so fond of horses. What are you going to do about it? You can't let them starve.

JOHN (*as he moves above the settee to* R) Of course I can't! I'll have to fork out, that's all. But when is it going to stop? The man's obviously toxic—liable to get carbuncles on his backside every other month.

STELLA. No, dear, I remember reading about it—they never strike twice in the same place.

JOHN (*as he looks at the bits and pieces on the settee*) What's all this mess?

STELLA. I had a sandwich.

(JOHN *looks at her*)

It wasn't very nice.

JOHN. That's quite obvious. Apparently you filled your mouth with liver sausage and blew it all over the settee. (*He takes up a half cigarette from the ashtray*) "Le petit Caporal". (*He looks at Stella surprisedly*) French.

STELLA. How clever of you, dear.

(LINDA *hurries in through the archway and makes for the stairs. She carries Pat's semi-overcoat, a waist-length duffle-type in red and black check*)

JOHN (*to Linda*) What have you got there?

LINDA. It's Miss Pat's, sir. (*As she looks at Stella*) Oh, dear!

STELLA (*smilingly, as she moves up stage*) That's all right, Linda. (*Taking the coat*) You can get on with your work.

LINDA (*unhappily*) Yes, ma'am.

(LINDA *hurriedly exits through the archway as* STELLA *holds out the coat*)

STELLA (*laughingly, to John*) Have you ever seen anything so ridiculous? Pat sent it by post.

JOHN. From Paris?

STELLA. Yes. She wants it French cleaned.

JOHN (*moving down* R) I see. And I suppose you found the cigarettes in one pocket and the liver sausage in another? (*Abruptly*) She's here, isn't she?

STELLA. Yes.

JOHN. Why didn't you tell me at once?

STELLA (*putting down the coat*) You seemed so upset about Corinne—I wanted you to recover a little before hearing about Pat.

JOHN (*anxiously, as he moves below the settee to Stella*) Is she ill?

STELLA. No, dear.

JOHN (*quickly*) Has she left her husband?

STELLA (*quickly*) No, dear.

JOHN (*quickly*) Is she unhappy?

STELLA (*quickly*) No, dear.

JOHN (*quickly*) Does she want anything?

STELLA (*quickly*) Yes, dear.

JOHN (*quickly*) How much?

STELLA (*quickly*) Five hundred pounds.

(JOHN *slaps a hand to his forehead and collapses into the arm-chair* LC)

John, it could have been so much worse! She might have married a man who knocked her about.

JOHN. I see. So I'm to regard my daughter's marriage as highly successful just because she hasn't got a black eye.

(STELLA *forces a little laugh*)

I thought you told me Pat's husband was an established playwright.

STELLA. He is. It's just that he hasn't been established long enough.

JOHN. Has he ever had a play taken?

STELLA (*moving* RC) Of course he has. (*Turning*) But Peter doesn't *want* his plays to be acted. He's an Existentialist.

JOHN. What does that mean?

STELLA. He's fifty years ahead of himself.

JOHN. Good. He's obviously going a long way. (*He rises*) Would anybody have believed it possible? My two daughters. After devoting my whole life to them—after all my hopes and prayers that they would marry into safety and security—and I scarcely know the names of their penniless husbands. (*Angrily*) Damn it, I haven't even met them!

STELLA (*moving* C) Corinne was too scared to bring Barnaby here, and Pat had to signal from the window to let Peter know whether you were in or out. Can you wonder that they slipped away to get married?

JOHN. That's right! Blame me for it. The father's always in the wrong. Give the children money—and you spoil them. Don't give them money—and you handicap them. Expect much from them—and you set too high a standard. Expect nothing from them—and you give them an inferiority complex. There's no answer to it.

STELLA. Oh, but there is! Surely, as long as they're happy . . .

JOHN (*crossing to* R) Nonsense! Any monkey with a bomb tied to its tail can be happy until it goes off! Thank God Gwen is only sixteen. I'll make sure *she* meets the right man. (*Turning*) Why didn't Peter have the guts to come and ask me for that money himself?

STELLA. He couldn't get away.

JOHN. He could have phoned me.

STELLA. At the moment he doesn't happen to be on the phone.

JOHN. He could have written, he could have sent a telegram. No! He preferred to send his wife.

(*The door* L *is flung open and* PAT *enters*)

PAT (*almost shouting*) He did *not* send me! He doesn't even know I'm here.

JOHN (*staring at Pat*) Good God! Have you been ship-wrecked?

STELLA. John! That's not a very sweet welcome.

JOHN. But why has she disguised herself? (*To Pat*) What's happened to you?

PAT (*moving towards the stairs*) I can't stand any more questioning!

STELLA (*restraining her*) Pat, dear, your father's only interested.

PAT. He's not!

JOHN. I certainly am. For one thing, I'm interested to hear how you got that black eye.

STELLA. A French aristocrat hit her with a bottle.

JOHN. *What?*

STELLA. It was an accident—he didn't *know* he was doing it.

JOHN. Well, what the hell did he *think* he was doing?

STELLA. Oh, don't bother about unnecessary details. (*Moving Pat towards John*) Aren't you going to give your daughter a kiss?

JOHN (*after a second's hesitation*) Yes, of course. (*He moves to Pat and kisses her on the cheek. He looks at her*) Are you happy?

PAT (*grimly, with her hands in her trouser pockets*) Yes, very!

JOHN. That's good. (*He pats her arm*) That's fine. (*He moves away to R as with some attempt at breeziness he continues*) Stella tells me that Peter is a—er . . .

STELLA. A playwright, dear.

JOHN. No, no. There was another word.

PAT. An Existentialist?

JOHN. That's it. What exactly does that mean?

PAT (*immediately on the defensive*) Existentialism is a philosophy. It's a school of thought that seeks to reaffirm, in modern idiom, the stoic form of individualism.

STELLA. Isn't it exciting?

JOHN (*to Pat*) Are you sure you understand what you're talking about?

PAT (*defiantly*) Peter is teaching me to understand it.

JOHN. I see. And is that ridiculous get-up an expression of individualism?

PAT (*angrily*) Yes, it's exactly that! I *am* an individual now, with my own opinions and my own way of life.

STELLA (*restrainingly*) Pat, dear . . .

PAT (*losing all restraint*) But I don't expect *you* to appreciate that. Any more than I could expect you to appreciate a Leonardo da Vinci, or a Bach concerto, or anything else that didn't find its inspiration in the Stock Exchange. It must seem quite ridiculous to you that Peter doesn't write his plays for money.

JOHN. Not at all. As long as *I* keep my health and strength, why should he?

PAT (*livid*) I'll never forget that as long as I live. (*Loudly, as she turns and makes for the stairs*) Never! (*Hurrying up the stairs two at a time*) Never!

(PAT *exits up the stairs.* STELLA *moves* L)

JOHN (*hiding his upset*) Well, that was a pleasant little interlude. (*He moves to the whisky*) Quite like old times, wasn't it?

STELLA. She's on the verge of a nervous breakdown.

JOHN (*angrily, as he pours himself a drink*) Then why isn't Peter here to look after her, instead of gallivanting about in Paris?

(JOHN *drinks as* STELLA *replies*)

STELLA. He's *not* gallivanting about in Paris. He's in prison.

(JOHN *splutters, bangs down his glass on the table and moves to* c)

JOHN (*almost whispering*) *What* did you say?

STELLA (*moving to him*) John, dear, please take things calmly. I read somewhere the other day that this world is *not* the centre of the universe. Do remember that. I don't want you to have a stroke.

JOHN. This is no time to discuss my blood pressure! Deviating, for just one moment, it might interest you to know that the doctor says I'm below what I should be above. But that was before this morning! (*Managing to control himself*) Now then. What were you saying as to the whereabouts of my precious son-in-law?

STELLA. He's in a little prison—just a very small one—and it's only used for the nicest people.

JOHN. And what has he been charged with—murdering his six other wives?

STELLA. No, dear—he smashed up the *Petit Fish* Night Club —but he didn't do it with malice aforethought. He was sitting by himself, quietly drinking a cup of coffee, when somebody insulted the British Empire. Peter, of course, immediately lost his temper and went through the Club like a bulldozer.

JOHN (*pleasantly surprised*) Oh. Well, that's something to his credit. (*Moving* R) God knows we can do with an expression of patriotism these days. (*Turning*) I never imagined he was that sort of fellow.

STELLA. Oh, yes. He's terribly like that. And that's why Pat wants the five hundred pounds.

JOHN. You mean for compensation?

STELLA. Yes. Peter insists upon paying for the whole thing himself. As soon as he does, he's as free as the wind.

JOHN (*smilingly*) Tell Pat to come down and see me.

STELLA (*blowing him a kiss*) You're the sweetest man in the whole world!

(STELLA *turns, moves towards the stairs—and the telephone rings. She takes the receiver*)

Hullo? . . . Yes, this is Mrs Bentley speaking . . . Oh, yes, I've been wanting to meet him for weeks . . . Oh, no! Not this morning. You must stop him . . . (*Frantically*) But you don't understand! Would you hold on, please?

(STELLA *covers the mouthpiece with her hand and looks towards her husband, who is glancing at the "Financial Times"*)

(*Appealingly*) John, dear—go into the garden.

JOHN. Why?

STELLA. I *must* be left alone for just two minutes.

JOHN (*moving towards her*) Let me have a word.
STELLA (*hurriedly*) No, no. It's quite all right.

(STELLA *turns her back and huddles over the mouthpiece, and* JOHN *continues to read his newspaper as she continues at the phone*)

Hullo? . . . Er—parlez-vous français?

(JOHN *looks up*)

Bon. Alors, fait attention. (*Emphatically*) Il ne faut pas venez ici ce matin . . . Non! Mon mari est ici et il savez absolutely rien de tout . . . (*Appalled*) Il a departé . . . Ici dans cinque minutes? Oh, mon Dieu!

(STELLA *replaces the receiver and acts a happy laugh to* JOHN, *who acts one back*)

JOHN (*putting down his paper*) That was really quite extraordinary. I can't understand a word of French but I got the whole gist of that.
STELLA (*moving down* C) Did you, dear?
JOHN (*moving down* R) Why don't you want somebody to come round here this morning, and what is it I know nothing about?
STELLA. Would you like another whisky?
JOHN. Answer my question!
STELLA (*after a moment's hesitation*) It's Gwen.
JOHN (*moving in front of the settee*) What do you mean?
STELLA. She's in love.
JOHN (*irritably*) What are you talking about? She's only sixteen—she could still be at school.
STELLA (*moving to him*) John, please believe what I'm telling you. She's desperately—dangerously in love.

(*There is a pause.* JOHN *stares at Stella. Then he pulls himself together, takes a rigid and imposing stance and enquires heavily*)

JOHN. Who is the boy?
STELLA. Well, he isn't quite a boy, dear. I suppose he's a man, really.
JOHN. How old is he?
STELLA (*after a moment's pause*) Thirty-seven.

(JOHN *stares at her blankly for a moment, then he half closes his eyes and fumbles to loosen his tie as he collapses on to the settee.* STELLA *hurriedly sits* L *of him*)

Oh, John! Take some deep breaths or something. Think of the Milky Way—and all those stars. My book says they're not really there at all. (*Brightly*) Do you realize that at any moment the earth may lose its atmosphere? That would mean complete oblivion for everybody, including Corinne's cowboy, Pat's playwright, and—er—Gwen's crooner.

(JOHN *stares fearfully at Stella*)

JOHN. Gwen's *what?*
STELLA. He's a singer, dear. He croons into a microphone. He's the sensation of London! He's followed about wherever he goes—and even middle-aged women try to steal his braces as souvenirs. And he's absolutely original! Instead of making people happy—he makes them miserable. When he sings, he cries real tears! You can actually see them *streaming* down his face. It's wonderful! (*She rises and moves to her handbag at the* L *end of the settee table, as she continues*) And look at this. (*Producing it*) It's a press cutting I found in Gwen's bedroom last week.

(STELLA *holds out the press cutting and* JOHN *takes it*)

JOHN (*reading*) "Police were called to the stage door of the London Coliseum last night when three hundred devotees of Mr Bobby Denver screamed and fought to kiss his hand or tear a button from his jacket. There is no doubt about it, this tearful Romeo of Song—with little or no voice—has sobbed his way into the hearts of a million fans, one hysterical woman even going so far as to throw herself in front of the crooner's car and beg him to drive over her."
STELLA (*excitedly*) What do you think of it?
JOHN (*grimly, as he props himself up*) Has Gwen ever met this ghastly product of a degenerate age?
STELLA (*quickly*) Bobby says they've only met twice. He's staying at the Savoy Hotel, and one night I managed to speak to him on the phone.

(JOHN *surges to his feet and makes for the phone.* STELLA *turns, and moves up to* L *of the phone*)

What are you going to do?
JOHN (*lifting the receiver*) I'm going to send for the police!
STELLA. They'll give it to the papers. Anything to do with Bobby Denver and out comes a special edition.
JOHN (*slamming down the receiver*) My God, have we all gone mad? (*Crossing below Stella to* L) Years ago a man had to spend his whole life toiling upwards through the night, even having to die before he could make the slightest claim to fame. But in this enlightened epoch some silly so-and-so has only to coin a ridiculous catch phrase, or waggle his navel in front of a television camera, and within twenty-four hours he's practically immortal! (*Moving down* L *and turning*) Did I understand you to say he was calling here this morning?
STELLA (*moving down* C) Yes. His secretary said he was already

on his way. Any moment now—and you'll be able to discuss the whole thing with him as man to man.

John. I'll shoot him right between the eyes!

Stella. John dear, control yourself.

(John *holds his forehead and moves to sit in the armchair* LC)

John. Gwen, my baby daughter. (*Suddenly and angrily*) I blame *you* for this!

Stella. John!

John. For fourteen years you've tried to bring your mad stage world into the lives of my children, and this is the result.

Stella. What are you talking about? I gave *up* the stage to please *you!*

John. But you couldn't forget it, could you? Night after night, for years on end, you filled this house with actors and actresses. I'll never forget those evenings. It was a cold war with insanity. And when I couldn't stand it any longer, you went underground. Cunningly and ruthlessly you brought my daughters up to hate my way of life—and to hate the careers I had them trained for. And where are they now? Corinne and Pat married to improvident clowns, and Gwen in love with a weeper—a crooner.

Stella (*angrily*) I think you're forgetting that your first *wife* left you.

John (*irritably*) What's that got to do with it?

Stella. She left you because she couldn't stand your dull absorption with the City. Any more than Corinne or Pat could stand it. Any more than I can stand it! There's no colour in this house. No life, no sweet insanity! I'm sorry, John, but I've got to say it. I would willingly leave you tomorrow for either Laurel or Hardy.

John (*shocked*) You don't mean that?

Stella (*on the verge of tears*) Of course I don't. Oh, I'm sure everything will turn out all right—as long as we take things calmly.

John (*rising*) Thank you, Stella, I don't need advice. I know exactly what to do.

Stella. What?

John. Well, there's obviously something very much the matter with Gwen. I'm going to consult a psychiatrist.

Stella. I've already been to one.

John. When?

Stella. Two days ago. Gwen hadn't eaten for forty-eight hours, so I phoned my sister and she told me about a man called Hermann Schneider. He's a foreigner.

John. You surprise me.

Stella. He lives in a little flat at Park South, but he's frightfully clever. He once cured a woman who had fallen in love

with the high tides at Brighton. I told him about Gwen, and what
do you think he said?

JOHN. I haven't the faintest idea.

STELLA. He suggested we should try and get the crooner to
come and stay here.

JOHN (*ironically*) Did he really?

STELLA. He said that if Gwen could see him going to the bathroom to clean his teeth she would soon realize that he was just
an ordinary man like you or anybody else.

JOHN. Thank you very much.

(*There is an urgent ringing at the front door bell*)

STELLA. Bobby Denver!

JOHN. Now listen, Stella. I'm handling this my way. I don t
want any interruptions from *you*!

STELLA. I won't open my mouth.

(*The front door bell rings again as* LINDA *comes hurrying through
the archway*)

LINDA (*very excited*) Oh, sir, there's a crowd of people outside
the door, and somebody's ringing the bell.

JOHN (*irritably*) Well, go and open the door.

LINDA (*quickly*) But there are two policemen outside as well,
sir.

STELLA (*quickly*) It's all right, Linda. We have somebody very
important calling.

JOHN (*to Linda*) Take that plate away.

LINDA (*as she makes for the settee*) Very good, sir.

STELLA (*quickly*) And hurry! Mr Denver isn't used to being
kept waiting.

LINDA. Oh, ma'am! You don't mean Mr *Bobby* Denver?

STELLA (*quickly*) I certainly do.

JOHN (*to Linda*) Get a move on!

LINDA (*gaping incredulously*) Bobby Denver, the crying crooner?

STELLA (*irritably*) Yes!

(LINDA *moans, staggers, and collapses on to the settee*)

JOHN (*to Stella*) What's happened?

STELLA (*hurrying to Linda*) She's fainted!

JOHN. Damn it, why choose a time like this?

(*The front door bell rings again, as* JOHN *hurries to Linda*)

STELLA (*to John*) You'd better answer the door yourself.

JOHN (*indignantly*) I will not!

STELLA. Well, *somebody's* got to let him in.

(LINDA *opens her eyes and tries to prop herself up*)

(*To Linda; quickly*) Are you feeling any better?

JOHN (*immediately and emphatically*) Of course she is!

STELLA (*to Linda; quickly*) Do you think you can manage to answer the door?

JOHN (*immediately*) Of course she can! (*To Linda*) Come on. (*He lifts* LINDA *to her feet*) Ups-a-daisy!

(LINDA *sways like a reed in the wind*)

Now then. Best foot forward.

(JOHN *supports the staggering* LINDA *towards the archway as* STELLA *protests*)

STELLA. John, she can't!

JOHN. Of course she can. She's as steady as a rock.

(JOHN *releases* LINDA. *Swaying against the archway she clings desperately for support*)

Good girl, Linda. That's wonderful! Now then, steady as she goes.

(*With a mighty effort* LINDA *swings herself out into the passage and staggers out of sight*)

Splendid!

STELLA (*crossing to* L) She'll faint again when she opens the door.

JOHN (*returning from the archway*) Of course, I just don't understand your sex.

STELLA. I know, dear.

JOHN (*having glanced towards the french windows*) Damn it, now there's a bunch of old girls trying to climb over the hedge. (*Shouting towards the old girls*) Go away! Mind your own business! (*He closes the french windows*)

STELLA (*moving* LC) Shouldn't we tell Gwen to come down?

JOHN (*moving down* R) Absolutely no!

STELLA. Ssh!

(LINDA *appears, clinging to the archway*)

LINDA (*in a hoarse whisper*) If you please, sir—Mr Bobby Denver.

(*Laughing out loud,* BOBBY *surges into the room. He clutches a bunch of tulips and a full-length microphone with the flex coiled. His exquisite light fawn suit is torn in several places, his collar is open, his tie is missing, his hair is ruffled, he has no hat, there are lipstick marks on his cheek, and he is holding up his trousers. He moves* C, *as he says*)

BOBBY (*loudly and happily*) Hullo, Mrs Bentley! I suppose you are Mrs Bentley? Isn't it a lovely day? Phew! I thought I'd never make it. You know something'll have to be done about this popularity business. It's not safe to go out. (*Indicating John*) Who's this?

STELLA. My husband.

BOBBY. Well, well! (*To John*) I thought you'd be at the office. (*To Stella*) I hope you don't mind the mike coming in. I always take it with me—in case somebody asks me to sing.

JOHN (*moving to him; angrily*) Nobody's going to ask you to sing in this house!

STELLA. Oh, John, I'd love him to.

BOBBY (*smilingly*) That's very sweet of you.

STELLA (*indicating the microphone*) How does it work?

BOBBY. I'll show you. (*Holding out the microphone to John*) Hold it for a moment, will you?

(JOHN *reluctantly takes the microphone*)

That's right! (*To Stella*) Now, we just plug it in and—if it doesn't fuse—Bob's your uncle. (*Uncoiling the flex*) Have you *got* a plug here? (*Looking* L) Ah, yes! There we are. (*As he moves* L *to plug the flex into the power point*) Of course, I don't have to do all this when I appear in public. Still, it's all exercise. (*Having plugged in*) Now then. I think we're all set. (*Moving to* LC. *To John*) Er—just for safety, sir—would you mind pressing down the little switch at the top?

(JOHN *irritably presses down the switch.* BOBBY *continues*)

(*Smilingly*) That's right! (*Brightly*) Would you like to try it, sir?

JOHN (*angrily bellowing, with the mike right in front of him*) I'll do nothing of the sort!

(*The amplification frightens* JOHN *into a dither, as* BOBBY *rocks with laughter and moves to John to take the microphone and stand it near the piano, clearing the flex as he does so*)

(*Angrily*) Now listen to me, Denver!

BOBBY (*still laughing*) Just a moment. (*To Stella*) What can I do with these?

JOHN (*livid, as he points*) My own tulips!

BOBBY. Yes, I'm afraid so. Your front garden's in a hell of a mess. They shoved most of your daffodils into my car. It was a Girl Guide who pulled these up. Well, they're no use to *you* now, *are* they?

(BOBBY *looks towards* LINDA, *who is still gapingly holding on to the archway, and smiles as he holds out the flowers*)

(*To Linda*) Here you are, darling.

(LINDA *totters towards Bobby as she whispers*)

LINDA. Oh, no! You don't mean it?

BOBBY. Of course I do. (*He hands the flowers to Linda as he continues*) With love from me.

(LINDA *gives a moan and goes down like a shot pigeon.* BOBBY *bursts out laughing*)

(*To Stella*) You know—(*indicating Linda*) that sort of thing used to upset me terribly—but I'm getting so *used* to it!

STELLA. Well, I'm not finding it frightfully original. John, she's very in the way. Do take her outside or something.

JOHN (*livid*) I'll do nothing of the sort!

STELLA. Well, I can't lift her, and if Bobby tries she'll probably have hysterics.

JOHN (*as he moves to Linda*) Hell and damnation! (*As he slightly raises* LINDA) You stay exactly where you are, Stella.

(JOHN, *walking backwards, drags* LINDA *towards the archway as he glares at Bobby and growls*)

And I've something to say to you, sir, when I come back.

(JOHN *exits backwards through the archway and the unconscious* LINDA, *still clutching the tulips, trails out after him*)

BOBBY (*laughingly, as he moves to* R) Very excitable, isn't he?

STELLA (*moving* C) Not as a rule. Would you like a drink?

BOBBY. No, thanks. I've only just had breakfast.

STELLA. Well, please sit down.

BOBBY. I can't. I'll have to be going in a moment. (*Looking at his wrist-watch*) The whole of the British Broadcasting Corporation is waiting for me. Doesn't it sound important?

STELLA. Very.

BOBBY (*moving* RC) I just can't get used to it. A couple of years ago I didn't even have to pay income tax. Now I owe them *thousands.* (*He laughs out loud, and suddenly grabs at his waistline*)

STELLA. Something gone wrong?

BOBBY. I can't keep my pants up.

STELLA. Don't you wear braces to hold them up?

BOBBY. I do as a rule, but the Girl Guide got those. (*He produces and holds out a pair of black silk braces from his jacket pocket*) I got them back, though. I did a half Nelson on her flag pole.

(STELLA *laughs as she moves to* BOBBY *and takes the braces*)

STELLA. Shall I help you?

BOBBY. You can't, darling. I've only got one button left. I lose about forty a week.

(STELLA *and* BOBBY *laugh, and* BOBBY *tightens the waist buckles of his pants as* JOHN *comes galloping back through the archway. He skids to a stop and glares at Bobby*)

JOHN (*moving* LC) What are you laughing at?

BOBBY. I've lost my braces again.

(JOHN *glares at the still laughing* STELLA, *sees the braces in her hand and gasps*)

John. Stella!

(Bobby *and* Stella *rock with laughter*)

Stella (*to John*) Oh, no! You don't understand!

(Stella *starts laughing again and* Bobby *doubles up with laughter as he totters to Stella. He tries to speak but only gurgles can be heard as he points to John, then to Stella, then to the braces, then to himself*)

John (*losing his temper; to Stella*) Pull yourself together! Are you crazy? Laughing like a stupid schoolgirl—when my daughter's morals are at stake.

Stella (*handing the braces to Bobby*) John, don't be so ridiculous!

Bobby (*shoving the braces into his pocket*) What's he talking about?

Stella. I've told him about Gwen.

Bobby. So what? The poor kid hasn't done anything wrong.

John. Are you trying to pretend you don't know she's in love with you?

Bobby. Dozens of women are in love with me—or *think* they are.

John. Gwendoline is not a woman. She's an innocent child. Damn it, you're old enough to be her father!

Bobby. So is Donald Peers. And what about Pappy Crosby— all the kids are in love with *him*. I can't help it if the whole sex has gone potty.

Stella. I think it's a lot to do with the food we eat—there's no *nourishment* in it.

John (*angrily*) Will you be quiet? (*Unbelievingly; to Bobby*) Do you mean to say you haven't encouraged this—this illicit infatuation?

Bobby. *Encouraged* it? I'm fed to the teeth with it! Gwen has twice forced her way into my dressing-room—and twice I've had her turned out. I spoke to her like a Dutch uncle—I wouldn't have bothered to do that if I hadn't liked the kid. Yesterday I received a telegram from her in which she said she would commit suicide if I didn't meet her alone for at least two minutes. I thought it time to come and see her mother.

Stella (*smilingly; to Bobby*) Her stepmother.

Bobby (*smilingly*) Of course—I should have guessed . . .

John (*pompously, as he raises his voice; to Bobby*) May I ask why you didn't prefer to interview her *father*?

Bobby. Because I've had previous experience of this sort of trouble, and I've never yet met a father capable of understanding any daughter.

(Gwen, *still wearing her dressing-gown, appears at the top of the stairs*)

JOHN (*to Bobby*) Have *you* any children?

BOBBY. No. I had a wife, but she left me.

GWEN (*from the stairs*) Why did she leave you?

STELLA (*turning*) Gwen!

(GWEN *descends the stairs*)

BOBBY. Oh. Hullo.

JOHN (*to Gwen*) Go back to your room at once!

(GWEN *moves to Bobby*)

GWEN. I saw you arrive, and my heart nearly stopped. Why have you come here?

BOBBY. Well—er . . .

STELLA. I asked him to.

GWEN (*to Bobby*) Why did your wife leave you?

JOHN. That's got nothing to do with you. Now listen, Gwen. This nonsense has got to stop. Denver himself has asked me to put an end to it.

GWEN (*to Bobby*) Have you?

BOBBY. I do think you're behaving rather foolishly.

JOHN (*to Gwen; angrily*) Damn it—(*pointing to Bobby*) he's nearly as old as I am! You're only sixteen!

GWEN (*to John*) Juliet was only fourteen when she fell in love with Romeo.

JOHN. They were foreigners!

GWEN (*to Bobby*) Cleopatra was only eighteen when she fell in love with Antony.

BOBBY (*to Stella; laughingly*) Some of the Cleopatras *I've* seen have been at least forty.

GWEN (*to John*) John Knox was fifty-nine when he married a girl of fifteen. Ruskin was forty-two when he fell in love with Rose la Touche, and she was only twelve.

JOHN (*angrily*) Denver isn't in love with *you.*

GWEN. I know, but I'm in love with him.

BOBBY (*to Gwen*) Now listen, don't be a silly kid.

GWEN (*quietly*) Why did your wife leave you?

BOBBY. We were temperamentally unsuited. She had no sense of humour. I used to knock her about. It was the only way I could make her laugh.

JOHN (*to himself*) Good God!

GWEN (*to Bobby*) You could never make me believe that. Oh, Bobby! I love you so much.

JOHN (*angrily*) Be quiet!

STELLA. Gwen, dear—not in front of your father.

GWEN (*to Bobby*) I fell in love with you that first Monday at the Coliseum. You sang—my favourite of all your songs— "Please don't forget to remember!" And you cried real tears. I've loved you ever since.

JOHN (*loudly*) Gwen! (*As he points*) Upstairs!

GWEN (*whipping round, angrily*) You can't talk to me like that! I'm not a child any longer.

JOHN. I'll talk to you as I think fit. Go to your bedroom.

GWEN. Bobby! Sing that song to me now. I'll listen to you from upstairs. Please, Bobby, sing it! I'll kill myself if you don't!

JOHN (*to Gwen*) If you stay down here two seconds longer, I'll put you across my knee. I've half a mind to do that, anyway.

GWEN (*as she stares wide-eyed at her father*) You've insulted me in front of *him*! I'll never forgive that. But I'll make you sorry for it! (*She turns and hurries half-way up the stairs, then she stops for a moment. Loudly and tearfully*) I'll make you so sorry for it you'll wish you'd never been born!

(*In a flood of tears* GWEN *exits up the stairs*)

BOBBY (*anxiously; to Stella*) She won't do anything silly, will she?

STELLA. I hope not. (*Turning*) John, for heaven's sake go upstairs and apologize.

JOHN. Apologize! I'll do nothing of the sort!

STELLA. You know what an impulsive child she is. She might throw herself from the window.

JOHN. What?

STELLA (*urgently*) Hurry!

JOHN. Oh, damn and damnation! (*As he hurries up the stairs*) Gwen! Wait for Daddy! (*Over his shoulder*) You stay exactly where you are, Stella!

(JOHN *exits up the stairs*)

BOBBY. Do you think she *will* throw herself from the window?

STELLA. No. She always talks like that when she wants to frighten her father. Besides, her bedroom used to be the nursery —it still has bars across the window.

BOBBY (*laughingly*) Doesn't *he* know that?

STELLA (*laughingly*) He's forgotten.

(JOHN *suddenly appears at the top of the stairs. He frantically descends two of them, as he shouts*)

JOHN (*desperately*) Denver! You'd better sing that damn nonsense. She's having hysterics in the bathroom!

(JOHN *tears up the stairs again and exits, as* STELLA *says*)

STELLA (*to Bobby*) There's the piano.

BOBBY. No! It upsets me too much. I'm not fit to meet anybody for hours afterwards.

STELLA (*as she makes for the stairs*) I'm not thinking of you— it's Gwen I'm worried about.

BOBBY (*moving to the piano*) Oh, damn it! (*Turning*) I'll have to use my microphone.

STELLA (*turning*) You won't need it in a little place like this.

BOBBY (*as he sits at the piano*) You'll be surprised.

(BOBBY *strikes some opening chords, then plays and sings with exaggerated tenderness and sentiment, with a choke in almost every note and conveying the impression that at any moment he will completely break down and sob his heart out*)

> The day we met, the roses grew
> And smiled at us, as if they knew,
> Alas, that roses die
> And we must say good-bye
> But—
> Please don't forget to remember
> Darling mine,
> Sweetheart, I didn't know
> How quickly those hours would go
> Since first I kissed your
> Lips so red
> You made my life divine,
> So please don't forget to remember,
> Darling mine.

(*Choking with sobs and apparently scarcely able to see for tears,* BOBBY *rises, chokes his way to the arch, turns his contorted and blear-eyed face to Stella, waves a feeble good-bye, then bursts into uncontrolled sobbing and exits.*

STELLA *herself is sniffing and dabbing a handkerchief to her eyes, and as* BOBBY *exits and* JOHN *appears at the top of the stairs she calls out*)

STELLA (*moving towards the archway*) Bobby! You can't leave like that!

JOHN. I hope he can! I've never heard such a damned awful noise in the whole of my life!

STELLA (*loudly*) Oh, do be quiet, you silly, dull man!

JOHN (*at the foot of the stairs*) Stella!

(STELLA *has already hurried to the piano. She grabs her hat and the beautiful roses that she had bought for her husband and makes for the archway as she calls again*)

STELLA. Bobby! Bobby! Wait for me!

(STELLA *exits through the archway as* JOHN, *bewildered and furious, moves to* C.

The french windows open and LINDA *enters carrying Mr Skeffington*)

JOHN (*immediately; to Linda*) What the hell do you want?

LINDA. I'm worried about the dog, sir. I was listening to Mr Denver singing and suddenly Mr Skeffington was sick on the crazy paving.

(JOHN's *face lights up. He delightedly pats the dog's head, as he exclaims*)

JOHN. There's a good boy! Good old boy!

CURTAIN

ACT II

SCENE I

SCENE—*The same. About four hours later.*
The settee has been tidied. The french windows are open. The sunlight shines from a different angle. On the settee is a black homburg. Bobby's mike is still plugged in and is standing near the keyboard of the piano.

When the CURTAIN *rises the stage is empty. A moment—and* LINDA *hurries in through the archway and makes for the stairs. She carries a glass of milk on a tray. She has hurried half-way up the stairs when the phone rings. She stops, turns, descends the stairs, rests the tray on the drinks table and takes the receiver.*

LINDA. Hullo? . . . (*Irritably*) No, it *isn't* Euston Station. You ought to know that by now.

(LINDA *replaces the receiver, hurries to the stairs and gets half-way up when she realizes she has left the glass of milk behind. She stops, turns, hurries down the stairs, takes up the tray, turns again, hurries to the stairs and is half-way up when the phone rings. She stops, turns, descends the stairs, rests the tray on the drinks table and takes the receiver*)

Hullo? . . . Oh, Mrs Bentley, where have you been? . . . Oh, but you don't know what's been happening! About two hours after you left, Miss Gwen jumped out of the bathroom window! . . . I'm not being silly, ma'am. We've had to have the doctor! . . . Yes, I found her myself, all unconscious, just by the dustbin . . . No, the doctor said she hadn't broken anything—but she's shaken everything up . . . Poor Mr Bentley's been nearly off his head with worry. He was so afraid she might try it again, he sent for that psychologicalist . . . Yes, that's right, ma'am—Mr Schneider, from Park South—he's upstairs with her now—and he's very worried about her. He says that when people deliberately jump out of a window, it usually means they've done it on purpose . . . Speak to who? . . . I'm afraid you can't, ma'am. Mr Bentley's gone to the chemist with the doctor's prescription . . . Oh, yes, please do, ma'am—as soon as you can! . . . Good-bye.

(LINDA *replaces the receiver, takes up the tray and hurries to ascend the stairs. She is half-way up when* JOHN BENTLEY'S *voice is heard*)

JOHN (*calling; off*) Linda!
LINDA (*stopping, turning and descending*) Yes, sir?

27

(JOHN *enters through the archway. He carries two medicine bottles wrapped in paper*)

JOHN. Who was on the phone?
LINDA (*at the foot of the stairs*) Mrs Bentley, sir.
JOHN. Where was she speaking from?
LINDA. The French Embassy, sir. I told her about Miss Gwen and she's coming right back at once.
JOHN (*as he places the bottles on the settee table* RC) She needn't bother.
LINDA (*unhappily*) Oh, dear!

(LINDA *starts to ascend the stairs as* JOHN *enquires*)

JOHN. Is Mrs Pember still upstairs?
LINDA (*turning at the second stair*) Yes, sir—so is Mr Schneider.
JOHN. What have you got there?
LINDA. A glass of cold milk for Miss Gwen, sir.
JOHN. The doctor said hot milk.
LINDA (*leaving the stairs*) I'm sorry, sir.
JOHN. And, Linda . . .
LINDA. Yes, sir?
JOHN. I don't want any talk about today's events. You understand?
LINDA. I won't whisper a word, sir.
JOHN. Good.

(LINDA *hurries away through the archway.*

JOHN *moves towards the stairs, stopping suddenly as he sees* MR HERMANN SCHNEIDER *solemnly descending them.* SCHNEIDER *is about fifty-five, short, stout: wild, curly hair, pale fat face and fierce eyebrows. His expressive hands are clasped behind his back and his head is bent in thought.* JOHN *asks anxiously*)

Well?
SCHNEIDER (*having reached floor level*) Mr Bentleys, ven ze doctor examine your daughter, did 'e find any bruises?
JOHN. I don't really know. He said she hadn't hurt herself. Why do you ask?
SCHNEIDER. Nussing. I vos joose vondering.
JOHN (*anxiously*) Mr Schneider, do you think she's going to be all right?
SCHNEIDER. Oh, yes. I don't sink you 'ave anysing to vorry about—except per'aps joost keep ze vindows closed. (*Turning*) Vy did you phone for *me*?
JOHN (*moving* C) My wife told me she had already seen you about Gwen.
SCHNEIDER. Ah, yes. I remember. Ze trouble is still viz ze same crying crooner?
JOHN. Yes.

SCHNEIDER (*moving to* L *of John*)   Zey are a nuisance, zose men—but an interesting phenomenon.

JOHN.   How do you mean?

SCHNEIDER.   Zey are cardboard lovers for disappointed vives—safety valves for respectable spinsters. Viz ze crooner on ze stage, ze ladies can go to ze theatre and have a little romance wizout getting into trouble. But wiz your daughter it is different. Zere is som'sing unusual. You are qvite certain you don't like 'im?

JOHN.   Quite!

SCHNEIDER.   I suppose zat is to be expected. After all, you are natural enemies.

JOHN.   Oh? Why?

SCHNEIDER (*shrugging his shoulders*)   Bobby Denver make ze people cry wiz 'is sad songs—you make zem laugh wiz your funny jokes from ze Stock Exchange. (*Briskly*) Tell me, you are not biased because of Mrs Bentley running after 'im?

JOHN (*moving to the* L *end of the settee*)   Not at all. My wife used to be an actress. I regard her behaviour this morning as just a piece of theatrical nonsense. It's Gwen I'm worried about. She's only a child.

SCHNEIDER (*moving down* C)   Ze female of ze species is never a child. A little girl is a small voman.

JOHN (*irritably*)   I don't wish to go into any unpleasant psychological ramifications. I live an ordinary decent life and I just want to know how to *deal* with this trouble.

SCHNEIDER (*briskly*)   Okay. I vill tell you. (*Sitting in the armchair* LC) But zis is positively my last professional appearance as a psychiatrist.

JOHN (*sitting on the settee*)   Oh. Why?

SCHNEIDER.   Mr Bentleys, my profession has been underminded by frivolous people. (*Angrily*) In every play in ze Vest End, zere is a psychiatrist! Zose damn playwrights! Zey 'ave look up our sleeve and put all our cards on ze table. (*Tearfully*) For six years, at Ellis Island, I study for my American degree—und in ze last six munce, I am almost bankrupt! For the future I will apply my psychological knowledge only to business.

JOHN.   But how does all this concern my daughter?

SCHNEIDER (*rising; excitedly*)   I vill tell you. (*Sitting on the settee,* L *of John*) My son 'as invented a silent—'ow you say?—der Behälter—der Behälter for *das Waschzimmer*—a silent cistern for ze little room.

(*There is a pause.* SCHNEIDER *looks at* JOHN *who blankly looks back at him.* SCHNEIDER, *seeking to elucidate matters, gives two little pulls at an imaginary chain*)

JOHN (*immediately, as he makes to rise*)   For heaven's sake!

SCHNEIDER (*stopping* JOHN *from rising*)   No, please! Listen! You

B

do not appreciate. (*Dramatically*) Instead of all ze "Yah, Yah, Yah!" ven ze vater pours from ze tank—zere is only a little "Sob, Sob, Sob"—like somebody crying. (*Briskly*) Now zen! For som'time, my son 'as vondered vot to *call* ze silent cistern. But today, I can tell 'im! (*Excitedly*) Ve vill call it ze Bobby Denver!

JOHN. Oh, ridiculous! (*Rising*) I'm sorry. I'm very busy. (*He moves* R, *then above the settee table*)

SCHNEIDER (*rising and moving* LC) Too busy to bozzer about your daughter's happiness?

JOHN (*irritably*) How can such nonsense possibly concern my daughter or anybody else?

(SCHNEIDER *turns, then solemnly moves to* L *of John*)

SCHNEIDER. Mr Bentleys, ven a man accidentally shoot 'imself in ze heart—zat is tragedy, you cry. But ven a man accidentally shoot 'imself in ze seat of ze pants—even zo 'e die—you laugh. (*Forcibly*) It is ze same tragedy, but you laugh! Shall I tell you vy? (*Emphatically*) Because ze tragedy 'as been robbed of dignity. Do you see vere I am getting at? 'Ow could your daughter take seriously ze tragic tears of a man whose name vos on der Behälter for das Waschzimmer? It vill kill 'im viz ridicule! Und, at ze same time, ze publicity vill make much money for my son. (*Smilingly*) Ze perfect marriage between psychology and business.

JOHN. It would certainly make my wife change her mind.

SCHNEIDER (*smilingly moving to* LC) For zat reason also, I took ze liberty to phone Bobby Denver and ask zat 'e kom 'ere at vunce.

JOHN. Of all the damned impertinence! (*Moving* C) How did you know where to find him?

SCHNEIDER. Mrs Bentley tell me 'e live at ze Savoy. I phone zere und zey say 'e is at ze B.B.C. I phone again und—vunderful! —I speak to 'im personal.

JOHN. You didn't tell him about Gwen jumping?

SCHNEIDER. Oh, no! I only say som'sing very serious 'as 'appen und 'e is to kom at vunce.

JOHN. I won't see him. I'll throw him out!

SCHNEIDER (*solemnly*) Mr Bentleys, upstairs your daughter lies in her bed wiz her pillow wet wiz tears as she cries "Bobby! Bobby!" Please—don't keep 'im away from her. Ven a man is going to stab you in ze back—look him in ze face.

JOHN. Schneider, I'm quite convinced that you're an impostor!

SCHNEIDER (*indignantly*) Ich verstehe nicht!

JOHN. But I think you're a clever one. And if, by fair means or foul, you can put a stop to my daughter's infatuation for this crooner, I'll give you two hundred pounds.

SCHNEIDER. Soch money!

JOHN. Well? What do you suggest?

SCHNEIDER. I 'ave already explain ze Behälter for das Wasch-zimmer.

JOHN (*irritably*) No, no! I want something more definite.

SCHNEIDER. Okay. (*Briskly*) I vould advise zat—to prepare ze ground—you do ze rough stuff. Smack ze daughter, 'it ze vife. Make zem afraid of you.

JOHN. I'll do nothing of the sort.

SCHNEIDER. Ve sink of som'sing else. Tell me, vot is Bobby Denver's reaction to zis romance?

JOHN. He says he's not interested.

SCHNEIDER. Zen appeal to 'im to 'elp you. Ask 'im to do ze David Garrick.

JOHN. What does that mean?

SCHNEIDER. Vell, 'e deliberately drinks—to make ze daughter disgusted viz 'im.

JOHN. Have you any other ideas?

SCHNEIDER. For two hundred pounds? I didn't started yet. I sink it vould 'ave a great reaction on ze respect of your family—if you leave 'ome.

JOHN (*irritably*) What are you talking about?

SCHNEIDER. Eizer ze daughter gives up zis nonsense or you pack your bag und valk out—never to return!

JOHN (*moving* RC) I couldn't leave my home. My conscience wouldn't let me. Besides, I'm nervy about damp sheets.

SCHNEIDER (*clutching his forehead*) Mein Gott! At such a time. (*Suddenly*) Ah! (*Slowly, as he moves closer*) 'Ow vould ze wife react if, vun day, you bring 'ome—a strange voman?

JOHN (*indignantly*) Are you suggesting immorality?

SCHNEIDER (*emphatically*) If it is necessary zat you sacrifice yourself for zis great cause, I vould say, "Stop at nussing zat does not make you look foolish!" But I suggest only zat you change your way of living. Srow aside your British conventions and restraints! Your family laugh at zem. I am qvite certain zat it is reaction to your respectable solidity zat 'as make your daughter fall in love wiz ze Bohemian crooner. Okay! From today forwards, you vill live in soch a vay zat vill make Tou-louse-Lautrec seem like ze Salvation Army.

(*The front door bell rings urgently*)

Bobby Denver!

JOHN. Hell!

SCHNEIDER. Are ze vindows closed upstairs?

JOHN (*moving round the* R *end of the settee*) Yes, I think so. Where's that bromide? Ah! (*As he takes up the bottles*) D'you think I can give her a double dose?

SCHNEIDER. You should 'ave ask ze doctor.

JOHN (*as he hurries up the stairs*) I'll risk it.

(JOHN *exits up the stairs*)

SCHNEIDER (*to himself*) A double—a double. Now vot does zat remind me of? (*Suddenly*) But of course!

(SCHNEIDER *makes for the whisky and pours himself a treble as he happily hums a little tune.*
PAT, *still in her Existentialist garb, enters and descends the stairs. She is wearing large dark glasses and carries a book.*
SCHNEIDER *raises his glass and beams at the contents*)

Mr Schneider, 'ere's vishing you very 'appy complexes.

(*About to drink, his eyes open wide as* PAT *silently passes in front of him to exit through the french windows*)

(*Fearfully*) Oh, no! Mein Gott!

(SCHNEIDER *hurriedly drinks his whisky and mops his forehead with his handkerchief as* BOBBY DENVER *staggers in through the archway carrying a half unconscious* LINDA *over his shoulder.* BOBBY *is wearing a different suit. It isn't damaged, but his collar is open and askew. He carries his tie and his hat*)

BOBBY (*as he enters*) You know, this woman should only walk about in a bath chair.

SCHNEIDER (*moving above the settee*) Tell 'er to go back to ze kitchen.

BOBBY (*propping* LINDA *on to her feet*) She can't go anywhere. She's got paper legs. (*To Linda*) Are you feeling better?

(LINDA *feebly nods her head*)

Good. You know, I think it would be safer if you went about on all fours. Alternatively, answer the door with your eyes shut, then you won't know who's calling. *That* would help, wouldn't it?

(LINDA *feebly nods her head.* BOBBY *leaves go of her.* LINDA *sways sideways and* BOBBY *grabs her again*)

Listen, honey, you're in a bad way. I'd like to see you go to bed.

(LINDA'S *eyes open wide, she smiles, then goes down like a shot pigeon.* BOBBY *looks at Schneider*)

She misunderstood me.

(JOHN *comes hurrying down the stairs*)

(*Smilingly*) Good afternoon. (*He moves* L *and indicates Linda*) You're just in time.

JOHN (*livid*) No, by heaven, she can stay there!

BOBBY. It looks so untidy.

JOHN (*moving to Linda*) Hell and damnation!

(JOHN *glares at Bobby as he half lifts* LINDA *by the arms*)

I believe you do it on purpose.

BOBBY. As a matter of fact, I do. Your wife said you needed exercise.

(JOHN, *walking backwards, drags* LINDA *towards the archway as he glares at Bobby and growls*)

JOHN. I curse the day I met you!

(JOHN *exits through the archway with the still unconscious* LINDA *trailing after him, as* BOBBY *remarks*)

BOBBY (*to Schneider*) What a title for a song. (*Singing*)

I curse the day I met you . . .

SCHNEIDER (*ingratiatingly*) May I take your 'at?
BOBBY. Sure.

(BOBBY *holds out his hat. It has been torn right across and the two sections hold together by a thread. He moves* C)

Which half would you like?
SCHNEIDER (*moving to* RC) Oh, no! (*As he takes the hat*) 'Ow 'as it got broken?
BOBBY. The usual struggle. Another excited female. (*As he pulls a woman's stocking from his pocket*) But I'm hitting back! Oh, boy, I'm hitting back! (*As he shoves the stocking back into his pocket*) There's no telling what I might win in the next scrimmage.
SCHNEIDER (*excitedly, referring to the hat*) May I keep zis?
BOBBY (*as he puts his tie on*) If you like that style.
SCHNEIDER. Oh, sank you. I vill make a pair of Bobby Denver slippers wiz it. I vill sell zem. Ho, ho! (*As he shoves the hat into his pocket*) You vait und see.
BOBBY. I can't wait—I've got an appointment.
SCHNEIDER. All in good time, Bobby. But first, before Mr Bentleys' return, I 'ave a proposition to make. My name is Schneider—Professor Hermann Schneider. Plis—vould you allow me to 'ave your name inscribed on a Wasser Behälter?
BOBBY .That depends. Where's it worn?
SCHNEIDER. I refer to ze vater tank in ze—er . . .
BOBBY (*amazed*) You don't mean the thingummybob in the whatyoumaycallit?
SCHNEIDER. Exactly! It would be a sensational advertisement.
BOBBY. Certainly not!
SCHNEIDER (*turning nasty*) Okay. Zen I vill not use your name. I vill inscribe ze *Behälter*—"Ze Crying Crooner".
BOBBY. You know, you're hitting below the belt. I don't think I like you.
SCHNEIDER (*angrily*) I am a business man. I do not appreciate sentiment. To me, you are no more zan a little cog in ze veel of my ambitions.
BOBBY. So! You make ze insult, huh? You sink you can play

ze big shot, heh? Mein Gott! Ich möchte etwas Brot mit Booter und Kässe und dann einen Pfannkuchen!

(SCHNEIDER *angrily protests in a flow of ad lib. German.* BOBBY *angrily interrupts him*)

Horch! (*Menacingly*) If you put my name on ze pull sing I go to the polizei, und you get ein, zwei, drei, vier, *funf* years imprisonment. Und ven you kom draussen—I kick ze shins—und brechen das necken!

(*More angry ad lib. German from* SCHNEIDER, *and* JOHN *enters through the archway*)

JOHN (*angrily interrupting*) Schneider—shut up and get out!

SCHNEIDER. Danke schon! Auf wiedersehen!

(SCHNEIDER *turns, grabs his hat, and hurriedly exits through the french windows*)

JOHN (*moving to* L *of Bobby*) Denver, I quite appreciate that theatre people have a warped sense of humour—but this afternoon even *your* witticisms seem out of place.

BOBBY. Why? What's happened?

JOHN. Some two hours after you left this morning Gwen jumped from the bathroom window.

BOBBY. Are you serious?

JOHN. Of course I am.

BOBBY. But—I had no idea. Is she hurt?

JOHN. Fortunately, no. (*Moving* L) But I think it's high time you realized that her ridiculous infatuation is no laughing matter.

BOBBY. I never thought it was. What made her do it?

JOHN. She knew my wife had gone off with you.

BOBBY. You mean Gwen jumped out of the window because of—what was it, jealousy?

JOHN. If one can apply such a term to her unbalance, yes.

BOBBY. Good Lord! What can we do about it? I'm as worried as you are.

JOHN (*returning to* L *of Bobby*) Listen, Denver—for some fantastic reason Gwen regards you as an idealist. To her, your tears are an expression of spiritual emotion and poetic sentiment—and nothing I can say will alter that opinion.

BOBBY. Well, what do you suggest?

JOHN. You've got to disillusion her. You've got to do a Henry Irving—(*hurriedly*) I mean, a David Garrick. You've got to do something that will make her ashamed of you—and I'll be very obliged if you can manage to do it away from her—and away from me.

BOBBY. Times have changed, you know. When Garrick pretended to get tight, it was regarded as a social disgrace to have one over the eight.

JOHN. In my circle, sir, it still is.

BOBBY (*moving away* R) Ah—but you're not a Rotarian.

JOHN. As it happens, I am—and I've yet to see a member of the Club under the influence.

BOBBY. I must have joined the wrong branch.

(STELLA *enters through the archway.* JOHN *turns and moves* LC)

STELLA. Hullo, Bobby! What are *you* doing here? (*She removes her hat and places it on the table above the settee*)

BOBBY. I was sent for, urgently.

STELLA. Because of Gwen?

BOBBY. Yes.

STELLA (*moving down* C) John, did she really jump from the window?

JOHN (*coldly*) I would prefer not to speak to you. But as you are directly responsible for Gwen's mad impulse, I will advise you. Yes, she jumped from the bathroom. She whispered that information herself.

STELLA. Where was she found?

JOHN. Just by the dustbin—flat on her back, quite unconscious, her face wet with tears. (*Indignantly*) Are you smiling?

STELLA. Only with relief. (*Turning*) Bobby, will you excuse me?

(JOHN *immediately moves to the foot of the stairs*)

BOBBY. Of course, darling.

(STELLA *moves towards the stairs*)

JOHN (*to Stella*) I don't wish you to see her.

STELLA (*amazed*) What?

JOHN. She certainly doesn't want to see *you*. Quite apart from that, she's in a deep sleep. I gave her a double dose of bromide.

STELLA. Then I can see her without waking her.

JOHN (*emphatically*) I prefer that you remain down here.

STELLA. Will you please get out of my way?

JOHN. No, I will not.

STELLA. I'm going upstairs. If you try to stop me—I'll hit you.

JOHN (*shocked*) You'll *what*?

BOBBY. Oh, don't start any rough stuff.

JOHN. Ah, yes! (*Quietly, as he looks at Stella*) Rough stuff! (*Loudly*) Stella, sit down!

STELLA (*emphatically*) I'm going upstairs.

(STELLA *moves forward and* JOHN *gives her a gentle push on the shoulder—just enough to send her back one step*)

BOBBY. Oh, no!

(STELLA *has already recovered her balance and she gives* JOHN *a push in the chest that sends him staggering backwards, to land on his backside at the foot of the stairs*)

STELLA (*to Bobby*) I hope that hasn't distressed you too much?
BOBBY. It was fascinating.
STELLA (*moving down* RC) I've never done it before. It was quite spontaneous.

(JOHN *has risen. He moves down to* L *of Stella, as he says*)

JOHN. Your whole attitude makes me feel quite sick with disillusionment. Not content with an afternoon of shameful flirtation . . .
STELLA. Oh, John! Don't be so stupid. I had an innocent little fling and I feel all the better for it. Now I can settle down again and lose my personality without feeling restless. I think all wives should have a little fling now and then. (*To Bobby*) Don't you?
BOBBY. Well, it rather depends *who* they fling.
JOHN (*to Stella*) You were away for over four hours!
STELLA. But I wasn't with Bobby all that time. I spent an hour at the bank and two hours at the French Embassy. It may interest you to know that I got Peter released from prison at exactly three thirty. He's flying over on the first plane possible.
JOHN. He's not going to stay *here.*
STELLA. Oh yes, he is.
BOBBY (*to Stella*) Who's Peter?
STELLA. My son-in-law.
BOBBY. What was he doing in prison?
STELLA. Sitting on a jury.
BOBBY. How very uncomfortable.

(STELLA *and* BOBBY *laugh together*)

JOHN (*to Stella*) Are you absolutely heartless? Do you want Gwen to jump from another window?
STELLA. She hasn't jumped from the bathroom window yet.
JOHN. What do you mean?
STELLA. The greenhouse is directly underneath it—and the dustbin is round the corner. I think Gwen rather lost her bearings —unless, of course, a frightfully strong wind caught her in mid-air.
JOHN. We shall see.

(JOHN *moves to the stairs and pompously ascends them to exit, as* STELLA *says*)

STELLA. Don't go, Bobby. (*As she hurries up the stairs*) We might have some *more* rough stuff in a minute.

(STELLA *exits as* BOBBY *replies*)

BOBBY (*following to the foot of the stairs*) Charming! I haven't enjoyed so much domesticity since my wife slapped me on the stomach with a cold hot-water bottle—and it was a stone one.

(*The telephone rings—just behind* Bobby. *He starts violently and takes the receiver*)

(*Into the phone*) Hullo? . . . (*In broad Scotch*) Aye, this is Euston Station . . . Aye, there's a train to Glasgow at six o'clock—but I'm afraid it went yesterday . . . Well, you maight faind a seat on the eight thirty express, but it's awful slow. I think you'll faind it quicker if you walk. Aye, and it's much cheaper . . . Well, if you've got to come back, I suggest you don't go at all—that'll be cheaper still . . . No, you can't get your threepence back. You've pressed Button A and it's a dead loss.

(*He replaces the receiver as* John *descends the stairs.*
John *passes Bobby without a word, moves to the archway and exits as* Stella *hurries down the stairs*)

Stella (*to Bobby, as she passes him*) We're going to inspect the dustbin.
Bobby. Have a nice time. (*He moves* LC)

(Stella *laughs and exits through the archway, as* Pat *enters through the french windows. She is carrying her book and wearing her dark glasses*)

Good Lord! I mean, hullo.
Pat (*stopping* R) Hullo.
Bobby. Who are you?
Pat. I'm one of the daughters here. Are you the crying crooner?
Bobby. That's right. But I don't think I could make *you* cry. What's your name?
Pat. Patricia. Why?
Bobby. I just wondered what sort of name went with those trousers.

(Pat *crosses to the stairs.* Bobby *continues*)

Are you Peter's wife?
Pat. Yes.
Bobby. I bet you're glad he hasn't got to sit on that jury any longer.
Pat (*turning, at the foot of the stairs*) What the hell are you talking about?
Bobby. I was only making conversation.
Pat. Listen, you've caused *enough* trouble in this house. Why don't you beat it?
Bobby (*moving to her*) What a pity!
Pat. What do you mean?
Bobby. You're so tough—and you *could* be so charming. You look like hell—and you could look so wonderful. (*He moves to the piano, as he continues*) A pretty girl shouldn't dress like that. (*He*

switches on the microphone and sits at the piano, as he continues) Don't
you want your husband to think—

(BOBBY *sings and plays—without fooling—" Sweet and Lovely ".
PAT *turns and starts to ascend* the stairs. *Almost immediately, she
stops and, without turning, listens—as* BOBBY *continues to sing.
Suddenly she turns*)

PAT (*interrupting wildly, as she turns*) Oh, shut up!
BOBBY (*stopping playing*) What's the matter?
PAT (*wildly, as she descends the stairs and moves down* C) Don't you
think I *want* to behave normally? (*She flings her book and glasses on
to the settee*) Don't you think I want to look like a woman? (*She
pulls off the red ribbon and shakes her hair loose*) I'm sick of this damn
way of living! (*Pulling off her jersey*) And I'm sick of these damn
clothes!

(*She flings her jersey aside. She is wearing a brassiere. Still in the
same wild mood, she fumbles angrily with the side zip of her trousers
as* GWEN, *in a dressing-gown, appears at the top of the stairs and*
BOBBY *rises and moves* C, *shouting*)

BOBBY (*to Pat*) Hi! Steady! That'll do.
GWEN (*from the stairs, to Pat*) You wicked *devil*!
PAT (*angrily, to Gwen*) Oh, go back to bed!
GWEN (*as she descends the stairs; to Pat*) I'll kill you! I'll kill you
in your sleep.
BOBBY (*to Gwen*) What's the matter with *you*?
GWEN (*moving to* L *of Bobby*) She was trying to seduce you.
(*Wildly; to Pat*) All right! Two can play at that game. (*She
wrenches at the cord of her dressing-gown*)
PAT (*at* R *of Bobby; to Gwen*) You crazy little fool! What are
you doing?

(GWEN *whips off her dressing-gown and flings it on the floor. She
is wearing pyjama trousers and jacket*)

GWEN (*to Pat*) Now then! It's *your* move!
BOBBY (*to Gwen*) You know, you need a damn good spanking!
(*To Pat*) So do you.

(BOBBY *picks up the dressing-gown and throws it to* GWEN)

Put that on at once!
GWEN. Not till she puts her jersey on!
BOBBY (*appealingly; to Pat*) Be a sport.
PAT. I'm not going to be dictated to by a silly kid.
BOBBY (*angrily*) You're sisters, aren't you?

(*He moves to* PAT, *grabs her by the wrist and pulls her towards*
GWEN)

Come on! You're going to kiss and be friends.

PAT (*struggling to release herself*) Leave me alone!

(BOBBY *holds her with difficulty as* JOHN *and* STELLA *enter through the archway to hear* BOBBY *shouting*)

BOBBY (*to Pat*) Damn it, one little kiss won't hurt you!

JOHN (*livid*) *What* did you say?

(PAT *wrenches herself free from* BOBBY *and he staggers back to near* GWEN, *who hurriedly puts on her dressing-gown as* PAT *picks up her jersey and* JOHN *moves forward to* C, *and* STELLA *moves down* R)

{*To Bobby*) I'll get you six years for this! But first I'm going to thrash the daylights out of you.

(PAT *hurriedly puts on her jersey as* GWEN *moves protectingly to the front of Bobby*)

GWEN (*on the verge of tears; to John*) Oh no, you're not.

JOHN. Get out of the way!

GWEN (*wildly*) I won't!

STELLA. John, there must be *some* explanation.

PAT (*to John*) Gwen and I had been rowing each other. He was asking me to kiss *her*.

STELLA (*to John*) There. You see?

JOHN (*to Pat*) Who removed your jersey?

GWEN. She removed it herself. She was trying to attract him.

PAT. I was not!

GWEN. You were! (*To John*) And, as a counter-measure, I removed my dressing-gown.

JOHN (*moving past Pat to Stella*) Now perhaps you'll realize the damnable effect these men have on women? (*Angrily*) I suppose I should feel flattered that you came home with your hat on.

BOBBY. Er—could *I* have a little word?

JOHN (*turning*) Not to me! (*Moving back to* C) I'm going to throw you into the gutter, where you belong.

GWEN (*desperately*) Daddy, if you touch him, I'll hit you!

JOHN. *What* did you say?

STELLA. John, you're being narrow-minded and biased. Personally, I think Bobby's a decent man and I like him.

GWEN (*wildly*) I love him!

(JOHN *looks hopefully at Pat*)

PAT (*to John*) He made me realize that I've been dressing like an idiot. I'm grateful to him.

JOHN. I see. (*To Stella*) It appears that I'm the only one with any sense of decency. (*Sorry for himself*) I feel rather in the way. Excuse me.

(JOHN *turns and solemnly ascends the stairs to exit*)

PAT. What's he going to do?

STELLA. I don't know. (*Moving to* c *and looking up towards the stairs*) I believe I'm rather worried.

BOBBY. He won't jump from the bathroom window, will he?

STELLA. I don't think so. He couldn't get through it.

GWEN. *I* did.

PAT. You did not!

GWEN. I did! (*Moving to* L *of Pat*) I landed on the greenhouse, fell to the ground, and staggered round to the dustbin.

PAT. Ha!

GWEN. I did! (*To Stella*) And if you go out with Bobby again, I'll jump from the roof. I'll jump from the roof every day until I'm dead!

BOBBY (*to Stella*) I don't think that bromide had much effect.

GWEN (*wildly, as she moves to him*) Oh, Bobby! I love you so much!

BOBBY. Oh, shut up!

STELLA (*suddenly*) Ssh! (*She looks towards the stairs*)

(JOHN *enters to descend the stairs. He is wearing his bowler hat and he carries a suitcase. It has obviously been jammed full of clothing in a hurry and one pyjama leg hangs out.* PAT *subdues a laugh, and sits at the* R *end of the settee*)

John dear, are you going somewhere?

JOHN. I'm leaving.

GWEN. Oh, Daddy!

JOHN. I no longer fit in with the scheme of things here. I don't feel bitter—just a little heartbroken, that's all. Do you happen to know where my umbrella is?

BOBBY. He's going to Manchester.

(STELLA *tries to control her laughter.* JOHN *stares at her with amazement*)

JOHN. Is nothing sacred to you? I may never see you again. Is there anything particularly funny about that?

STELLA (*at* RC) No, dear, of course not. It's just that—(*pointing to his suitcase*) your pyjamas are hanging out.

JOHN (*having glanced at his suitcase*) Ah, yes. I understand. My tragedy has been robbed of dignity. (*He looks from Stella to Pat and Gwen, then back to Stella*) Well, good-bye.

GWEN (*on the verge of tears*) Daddy! You can't leave us. What will we do?

JOHN. Oh, I'll make all necessary arrangements. I'll still look after you.

(BOBBY *quietly moves to the piano as* PAT *says*)

PAT (*to John*) Damn it, this is your home!

JOHN (*bitterly*) I have no home.

(BOBBY *switches on his microphone and sits at the piano, as* STELLA *replies*)

STELLA (*to John*) I never thought *you* would desert your family.
JOHN (*bitterly*) I have no family!

(BOBBY *sings and plays* "*High Noon*", *commencing with the request that he be not forsaken.* JOHN *freezes.* STELLA *tries hard not to laugh.* PAT *claps a hand to her mouth and shakes with suppressed laughter.* GWEN *bites her lip to stop crying, and sinks into the armchair* LC. BOBBY *tearfully continues singing.* JOHN *suspiciously glances from Stella to Pat to Gwen—and again at Stella. Then he carelessly shrugs his shoulders and moves to near Bobby—as much as to say "I can take it."* BOBBY, *tearfully continues singing.* JOHN *again shrugs his shoulders and carelessly meanders to the archway, as* BOBBY *continues.* JOHN *stands still in the archway, with his back to his family.* BOBBY *continues singing—and as he reaches the last line of his song—*JOHN *suddenly drops his suitcase, grabs his handkerchief and bursts out sobbing as he turns and totters to* STELLA *to be enfolded in her arms.* GWEN *sobs out loud and* PAT *flops on to the settee to hide her laughter in a cushion, as—*

the CURTAIN *falls*

SCENE 2

SCENE—*The same. About two hours later.*
    John's suitcase has been removed. The french windows are closed, the curtains are open. The outside lighting is dusk. The lounge lights are on.

As the CURTAIN *rises,* JOHN's *voice is heard from upstairs.*

JOHN (*off; angrily*) There's no need for you to go at all!
STELLA (*off*) I've got to look after Gwen, haven't I?
JOHN (*off; angrily*) Then keep her away from Denver!
STELLA (*off*) Oh, John! Don't you understand? Tonight she says good-bye to Bobby for ever.
JOHN (*off; angrily*) All right!

(*A door upstairs is slammed—and* JOHN *enters, to descend the stairs. He is dressed as before. He is in a violent temper. He descends two or three stairs then turns as he shouts towards upstairs*)

But I warn you, Stella—if you *do* go, you'll find me a very different man when you return!

(*The telephone rings.* JOHN *descends the rest of the stairs, moves forward, grabs the receiver and growls*)

Hullo? ... (*Angrily*) No, it is not! This is the Beachy Head Lighthouse!

(*He slams back the receiver as* LINDA *enters*)

LINDA (*nervously*) If you please, sir, there's a Mr Michael Kenley to see you.

JOHN (*moving* LC) Tell him to go to the devil!

LINDA (*towards the passage*) Will you come this way, please?

(MICHAEL KENLEY *enters and* LINDA *hurries away.* MICHAEL *is about twenty, good-looking, manly, and not particularly well dressed. He carries his hat and a newspaper*)

MICHAEL (*smiling*) Good evening, sir.

JOHN. What the hell do *you* want?

(MICHAEL *laughs*)

MICHAEL (*briskly*) I'm from the *Daily Record*, sir. We wondered if you would be good enough to advise us if there was any particular reason for Bobby Denver calling here twice today. We've had quite a number of phone calls about it—and we thought you might be able to give us some small piece of information that might be of interest to the general public.

JOHN. I loathe the general public—almost as much as I loathe people who force their way into my house to pick up bits of scandal.

MICHAEL (*brightly*) Scandal, sir? Ah! Now we're talking.

JOHN (*really curious*) Have you no shame?

(MICHAEL *laughs*)

MICHAEL. I was assigned to this job. I didn't choose it. Actually, I was on my way to attend a conference covering the recent statements of Italian scientists that there *is* life on other planets.

JOHN. Well, why didn't you go to it?

MICHAEL. The editor said Bobby Denver was more important.

JOHN (*piteously, as he holds his head*) Please go away! I feel desperately ill.

(PAT *enters to descend the stairs, as she says*)

PAT (*to John*) Why don't you go to bed?

MICHAEL (*as he looks at Pat*) Oh, gosh!

(PAT *is wearing a low-cut evening dress, with semi-crinoline to the floor—and she looks very beautiful and very feminine*)

JOHN (*smiling*) Ah! Now that *is* my daughter.

PAT (*as she leaves the stairs*) Thank you, Daddy.

JOHN. My dear, you look lovely. And the dress of course—I've never seen anything like it.

PAT (*moving* C) Yes, you have. Stella's been wearing it for over a year. (*Having noticed Michael*) Who's this?

JOHN (*irritably*) Nobody.

(PAT *immediately moves* RC *to shake hands with* MICHAEL)

PAT. How do you do?

MICHAEL (*smilingly*) Hullo.

JOHN (*to Pat*) Are *you* going to this damn television thing?

PAT (*moving* C) No. I'm going to Claridges. I'm meeting an elderly Guards officer who's the biggest snob in London. He'll probably make me sit at a separate table—but I'm going to enjoy every dull English moment of it.

(MICHAEL *laughs*)

JOHN. But what about your husband? He'll be here within half an hour.

PAT. That's why I'm going to Claridges.

JOHN. Pat, don't be so stupid.

PAT. Oh, Father! Do mind your own business.

JOHN. What?

PAT (*to Michael; as she moves to the archway*) You wouldn't get me a taxi, would you?

MICHAEL. You bet I would!

PAT (*with a smile*) Thank you.

(PAT *exits through the archway*)

MICHAEL (*to John*) Excuse me, sir? I'll be right back.

(MICHAEL *hurries away through the archway as* JOHN *shouts after him*)

JOHN. No, you damn well won't! If you ever look in here again, I'll break your neck!

(GWEN, *in evening dress, has entered to descend the stairs as she says*)

GWEN (*anxiously; to John*) Was that Bobby?

JOHN. No—but the same goes for him.

GWEN (*as she leaves the stairs*) Where's Pat?

JOHN. She's gone to Claridges.

GWEN (*wildly*) I don't believe it! Oh, damn and blast her, she's double-crossing again!

JOHN (*angrily*) If you use that language in front of me, I'll . . .

GWEN (*moving* LC) I'm sorry, Daddy—but she's *after* Bobby. I know she is!

JOHN (*moving* C) Well, I hope she gets him.

GWEN. But she's married!

JOHN. So is he! And it's about time you realized it.

GWEN. I've been realizing it all day. I'm not going to see him again after this evening.

JOHN. Where are you meeting him?

GWEN. He's calling for me here.

John (*moving to her*) Gwen, you're only a baby. Do you really want to flaunt yourself in front of all those people—with a married man of thirty-seven?

Gwen. I'm going to listen to him singing—and have a little supper with him, that's all. And—we're going to have a chaperon. Stella's coming, too.

John. That's what's worrying me!

(Linda *enters through the archway*)

Linda. If you please, sir—Mr Peter Pember.

John (*holding his forehead*) Oh, my God.

(Peter Pember *enters through the archway. He is a well-built fellow, about twenty-two. Crew-cut hair, and a beard of about a fortnight's growth. He is wearing clumsy yellow brogues, red socks and pale blue shorts: a brown sweater with a rolled neck, a mustard jacket, and a white beret. He carries a battered old suitcase, tied round with string—and a large paper parcel. He enters a step or two, then stands still and smiles sardonically at John*)

Peter (*moving c*) Hullo, Father.

(Linda *claps her hand to her mouth and hurriedly exits as* John *winces and closes his eyes*)

Gwen (*moving l*) Oh, no! (*To Peter*) You're not really Pat's husband, are you?

Peter. I hope so. I've been taking some awful liberties, if I'm not. Are you her sister?

Gwen (*aggressively*) Yes.

Peter. I don't think we're going to like each other.

Gwen. I know we're not!

John (*to Peter*) Take that bonnet off!

Peter. What do I do with my luggage?

John (*moving lc*) Well, if it belonged to me, I'd throw it away.

Peter. Jolly good idea. (*He throws the suitcase and parcel on to the floor above the r end of the settee and, without removing his beret, moves to c, as he produces a German-type pipe from his pocket. Brightly*) Where's my woman?

John. Your *what*?

Peter. My little one, my loved one, my rose of Sharon, my wife.

John. She's out.

Peter. Remind me to be annoyed with her. (*He fills his pipe with loose tobacco from his pocket as he glances round the room*) Well, well! So this is my new home. It simply reeks of Suburbia. But it has its memories. (*Smilingly; to John*) Months ago I used to wait for you to go to bed, then creep in here and do my courting. (*Looking rc*) Oh, how I remember that settee!

John (*moving to* L *of Peter*) I don't like your conversation, sir.

Peter (*producing a match from his pocket*) It isn't conversation, it's just idle chatter. I'm never very witty when I first meet people. I find it gives them an inferiority complex. (*He strikes the match on the seat of his shorts and lights his pipe*)

Gwen. Oh, Daddy! He's ghastly!

John (*to Peter*) Have you booked yourself in at a hotel anywhere?

Peter (*in between puffs*) No, dear boy, I'm staying here. Where my wife is, there am I—and let no man put asunder. (*He shakes the match out and throws it over his shoulder*)

John. Pember, I dislike you intensely!

(*Genuinely surprised,* Peter *looks at John and, at the same moment, exhales a mouthful of pipe smoke full into John's face.* John *chokes and coughs—then continues*)

If it hadn't been for the fact that you smashed up that Club in defence of the British Empire . . .

Peter (*interrupting*) What are you talking about? I don't *like* the British Empire.

John (*immediately; to Gwen*) Fetch your mother!

(Gwen *turns and hurries up the stairs to exit, as* Peter *says*)

Peter (*as he steps on to the settee*) *She* won't throw me out. She simply adores me.

John (*livid, as he moves to the settee*) Now listen to me, Pember . . .

Peter (*as he relaxes full length on the settee*) I'd love you to call me Peter.

John. I'll call you a lot of things before I'm through with you. Take your feet off that settee—and put that filthy pipe out!

Peter. Yes, I must admit it is rather offensive. It was given to me by a Swedish naturalist. A most charming fellow—I shared his cell. He'd been sentenced to six months for sitting his wife on a Primus stove—and he found the smell of this pipe just too nostalgic. (*As he takes them off*) Do you mind if I remove my brogues? I haven't had them off since last Friday.

John. Pember! I'm going to have you certified. (*He moves away to* L)

(Peter *puts his brogues on the carpet against the* R *end of the settee as he replies*)

Peter. My dear fellow, in this mad world, it would be a certification of sanity.

(Stella *enters to descend the stairs—in evening dress*)

Stella. Peter! How lovely to see you again!

PETER (*rising and stepping over the settee*) Ah, Stella! Charmante! Comment ça va?

STELLA (*leaving the stairs*) Tres bien, merci.

PETER (*as he takes her hand*) Est-ce que je peut vous embrasser?

STELLA (*moving* LC) Mais certainement!

(PETER *kisses* STELLA *on each cheek*)

(*Laughingly*) Oh, dear! You're quite Parisian, aren't you?

PETER. No, but I've picked up a lot of habits from the *English* in Paris.

STELLA (*laughing and turning to John*) John, dear, this is our son-in-law. Isn't he exciting? (*To Peter*) My husband's always very shy when he first meets people. You'll like him when you get to know him better.

PETER. I hope so. I must confess that up to now I've found him bitterly disappointing. (*He moves to flop on the settee*)

STELLA (*laughing; to John*) He's so witty. You mustn't be offended. He only says what he thinks. (*To Peter*) I'm afraid Pat had to go out.

PETER. So I understand. But why are you afraid?

STELLA (*laughingly*) Why have you taken your shoes off?

PETER. I'm giving them a breather. Do you like my socks? I knitted them myself.

STELLA. John—his socks!

JOHN. I've seen them!

STELLA (*laughingly*) Have you had anything to eat?

PETER. I'm still full of black bread from the prison.

STELLA. Well, you make yourself comfortable and I'll get you a nice big whisky.

JOHN. Oh, no, you won't!

STELLA (*moving* C) What do you mean?

JOHN (*with ominous restraint; as he moves to her*) Stella, you and I —in our different ways—have more or less enjoyed an association of some fourteen years. During that long time, I have given way to you on almost every conceivable occasion. But today, over the question of Bobby Denver, we have practically reached the point of separation. And if—to that crisis—you add the insult of allowing this indecent pathological specimen to stay in my house, then I most solemnly warn you, I shall not be responsible for my actions!

PETER. Very good!

JOHN (*continuing steadily; to Stella*) Don't be misled because I happen to be speaking quietly. Inside me, there is a seething beyond your understanding. I hear strange voices telling me to do things. There is a peculiar ringing in my ears . . .

(*There is an urgent ringing at the front door bell*)

PETER (*wiggling a finger in his ear*) *I've* got that.

(Gwen, *still in evening dress, and carrying a small fur cape, comes hurrying down the stairs to make for the archway*)

Stella (*to Gwen*) Where are you going?
Gwen (*excitedly*) It's Bobby!

(Gwen *hurriedly exits through the archway*)

Stella. Oh, John, it's Bobby!
John (*mockingly as he moves to the side of the piano*) Ow, it's Bobby!
Peter. Who's Bobby?
Stella. Bobby Denver, the crying crooner. Gwen's crazy about him. (*In a whisper, having glanced at John*) But he's thirty-seven and she's only sixteen.
Peter. Good Lord, that's nothing. I know an old farmer in the Pyrenees who married a girl of thirteen. He's *eighty*-seven. They both play with the same toys.

(Bobby *and* Gwen *enter together through the archway. She is holding his arm.* Bobby *is in full evening dress. There is no sign of any mauling from the fans. They move to* LC)

Stella. Hullo, Bobby!
Bobby. Hullo, darling!
John (*angrily*) You will not address my wife like that! I'm sick of your "darlings" to each other!
Bobby. It's only a theatrical expression.
Gwen. It doesn't mean anything, Daddy.
John (*moving* L) Get away from him! (*Pointing to the chair* L) Sit down there—go on!

(Gwen *crosses and sits in the chair by the door* L *as* Bobby *says*)

Bobby (*to Stella*) Quite a crowd outside—but look! No braces missing, no buttons ripped off. D'you think I'm slipping?
Stella. Perhaps they didn't recognize you in the dark.
Bobby. Well, that's insulting. (*Reacting suddenly and pointing as he notices Peter*) Who's this?
Stella. Er—Peter Pember, my son-in-law.
Bobby (*crossing to Peter*) How are you?
Peter. Why do you ask? You're not interested in my health.
Stella. He's an Existentialist.
Bobby. Oh, I see—wearing the national costume.
Gwen. Don't speak to him, Bobby. He's horrible.
Stella. Gwen!

(Peter *takes* Bobby's *right sleeve and pulls him on to the settee, as he says*)

Peter. As a matter of fact, Denver, we have quite a lot in common.
Bobby. Really?

PETER. Oh, yes. The morbid depression of your singing and the utter hopelessness of my philosophy form quite a strong link between us.

(BOBBY *rises and looks at Stella*)

BOBBY. I don't think I like him. (*Crossing to John*) Do *you* like him, Bentley?

JOHN. God forgive me, the appalling comparison has almost made me like you.

STELLA (*as she makes for the stairs*) Come along, Peter. I'm sure you want to have a wash or something.

(PETER *rises, steps over the* R *end of the settee, picks up his suitcase—not the parcel—and follows Stella*)

PETER. Am I sleeping with my wife?

STELLA (*as she ascends the stairs*) No. I'm afraid you'll have to have the little room next to my husband tonight.

JOHN. No, by heaven, he won't!

(JOHN *makes for the stairs. Finding* BOBBY *in his way he shoves him to one side, as* STELLA *exits and* PETER *follows.* JOHN *frantically ascends the stairs as he shouts*)

Stella! I've warned you. If he stays here, I'll cut his bloody throat. Stella!

(JOHN *exits as* BOBBY *laughs, and* GWEN *rises*)

BOBBY (*moving* C) You know, I believe your father's beginning to enjoy himself . . .

(*He stops, immediately apprehensive, as he notes the depth of feeling behind* GWEN's *steady gaze*)

GWEN (*quietly, as she moves to* L *of Bobby*) Hullo, my darling.

BOBBY (*nervously*) Gwen, you've got to be good.

GWEN (*quietly*) This is the first time, in the whole of our lives, that we've ever been left alone together.

BOBBY (*calling towards the stairs*) Stella!

GWEN. Oh, no!

BOBBY. Are you going to behave yourself?

GWEN. I promise. (*Crossing to the settee*) But please sit down—just for a moment.

BOBBY (*looking at his wrist-watch*) We've got to get to the studio.

GWEN (*appealingly*) Just until Stella's ready.

BOBBY. All right—but you stay where you are.

(*He sits in the armchair* LC. GWEN *smiles and sits on the settee. A pause. They look at each other.* GWEN *smiles and* BOBBY *immediately looks away*)

(*Briskly*) Tell me, how are you getting on at school?

GWEN. I've left school. Father's having me trained to be a secretary. I hate it! I want to be a writer. I want to write like Dostoevsky. (*Suddenly*) But I'd be *your* secretary. (*Rising and moving to near him*) Oh, Bobby, that would be a wonderful idea.

BOBBY. Forget it.

GWEN. Why did your wife leave you?

BOBBY. She made a hit on Broadway when I was still on the beach at Blackpool—few marriages could stand up to that.

GWEN. Where is she now?

BOBBY. In America.

GWEN. Do you still love her?

BOBBY. Yes.

GWEN. I hate her!

BOBBY. What an extraordinary child you are. Full of wild emotions. I suppose it's adolescence or something.

GWEN. Life itself is adolescent. In the great scheme of things, this old world of ours is very young.

BOBBY. Is that a quotation?

GWEN. Oh, no. I never express myself through the minds of other people. I'd rather kill myself.

BOBBY. There you go! Jumping out of the window again. Or *did* you jump?

(GWEN *ignores the question as she impulsively kneels beside him*)

GWEN. Bobby! After the television, let's give Stella the slip Let's have our little supper alone together.

BOBBY. No darn fear! (*Rising and crossing to* RC) Stella comes with us and Stella *stays* with us. And, after tonight, we don't meet again. That was what we arranged and you swore on your oath you'd keep to it.

GWEN (*rising*) Would you like a whisky?

BOBBY (*after a moment's pause*) Have you ever heard of David Garrick?

GWEN. No.

BOBBY. Then I'd like a large one.

GWEN. Oh, yes! I'll get it for you.

(*She hurries up stage to pour a large whisky as* BOBBY *sits on the settee*)

BOBBY. Nothing with it. I like it good and straight. I didn't have any for breakfast this morning and I'm rather missing it.

(GWEN *hurries to him with a glass full of neat whisky*)

GWEN. There you are, my darling.

(BOBBY *stares at the enormous drink, then takes the glass*)

BOBBY. Thanks.

(*He looks at the whisky—smiles feebly at Gwen—again looks fearfully at the whisky—unobtrusively crosses a couple of fingers, and drains the glass. His eyes bulge, his legs cross—and he is only just able to hold out the glass and gasp*)

May I have another?

GWEN (*excitedly, as she takes the glass*) Oh, please do!

(*She hurries to the radiogram and switches it on, then hurries to pour another glass-full as—unseen by her—BOBBY leans sideways with his hand on his stomach, and his face contorted. Suddenly, BOBBY's face brightens. He is looking down at Peter's big brogues. He half looks towards Gwen, then again at the brogues—and he sits up straight and smiles as GWEN comes back to him with the refilled glass*)

Are you sure you wouldn't like some soda water with it?

BOBBY (*happily, as he takes the glass*) Quite sure, thanks.

GWEN (*happily*) I'll get you a cigarette.

(*She turns and makes for the cigarette box on the piano, and BOBBY—having glanced towards Gwen—quickly pours the whisky into one of the brogues. He immediately tilts the empty glass to his lips as GWEN returns with the cigarette box—and quiet sentimental music comes from the radiogram*)

(*Holding out the box*) Help yourself.

BOBBY (*holding up his glass*) I'd rather have another whisky.

GWEN (*taking the glass*) Oh, good!

(*She hurries to pour yet another huge whisky and BOBBY has another peep at the brogues before continuing*)

BOBBY (*happily*) I'm afraid drinking is rather a strong weakness of mine. The doctor's trying to limit me to two bottles a day.

(*GWEN arrives with the whisky. BOBBY takes the glass*)

Hurray!

GWEN. Hurray, my darling.

(*She replaces the box on the piano and hurries to the foot of the stairs to look upwards and listen as BOBBY—having glanced towards her—hurriedly pours the whisky into the other brogue. GWEN turns from the stairs as BOBBY, with tilted glass, appears to be draining the dregs. She moves forward*)

(*As she gazes at him*) Oh, you don't know how I admire you.

BOBBY. What?

GWEN. For a man of your age to be able to drink nearly a pint of neat whisky in less than five minutes. I think it's wonderful!

BOBBY (*hopelessly*) You mean you're not disgusted?

GWEN. Of course not!

BOBBY. So much for David Garrick!

GWEN (*sitting* L *of him*) Why are you so cold and indifferent?
I thought the whisky would warm your heart.

BOBBY. Was that why you asked me to have a drink?

GWEN. Yes.

BOBBY. Of course, I just don't know what to do about you.

GWEN (*on the verge of tears*) I'm in love!

BOBBY (*rising*) Oh, don't talk nonsense! (*As he bangs his glass
down on the settee table*) Honestly, Gwen, I'm fed up with it. (*He
moves to the french windows and suddenly claps his hands to his eyes, as
he exclaims*) Aaaah!

GWEN. What's the matter?

BOBBY (*fearfully, as he slowly lowers his hands*) I've just seen the
new moon through glass!

GWEN. Don't be so old-fashioned.

BOBBY. Everything will go wrong with me now. I'm doomed!

GWEN (*rising and making for the french windows*) Well, I'm
going to be doomed with you.

BOBBY (*intercepting her*) No! Let me open the windows first.

(*He hurriedly opens the windows.* GWEN *moves to them*)

GWEN. Where is it?

BOBBY (*pointing*) There—just above the trees. Wish for something nice and ask it to let me off. (*He moves up* C)

GWEN (*looking out to the night*) Oh moon, serenely shining,
don't be unkind to Bobby. Turn his thoughts from primitive
superstitions and bring me closer to the man who is my love.
(*Suddenly as she steps back*) Oh!

(MICHAEL *enters through the french windows*)

MICHAEL (*to Gwen*) I'm sorry. I know I'm snooping—but
please let me in on this. (*To Bobby*) A little romance—yes?

BOBBY. Who are you?

MICHAEL (*crossing to* R *of Bobby*) I'm afraid I'm from the *Daily
Record*.

BOBBY. Well, what you heard just now is *off* the record.

MICHAEL. Okay, Bobby, if that's how you want it, but it
would mean a lot if you could give me some sort of angle.

BOBBY (*moving down* LC) Nothing doing. You report one word
of gossip and I'll get you the sack.

(MICHAEL *laughs*)

What's your name?

MICHAEL (*briskly, as he moves down* C) Michael—Michael
Kenley. Twenty-five years old. Born in Dublin. No parents. No
money.

GWEN (*moving down* R) A press reporter?

MICHAEL. Yes—but it won't last. I get kicked out of everything. (*To Bobby*) And I've just about tried everything. I've

washed up at Lyons, swept round at Selfridges, and last December
I was Father Christmas at Gamages. (*He laughs out loud*)

BOBBY. How do you manage to keep laughing?

MICHAEL. It started when I was Father Christmas and I can't
get out of the habit.

BOBBY. Are you married?

MICHAEL (*laughing*) Good Lord, no. Women don't take me
seriously.

BOBBY. Perhaps you don't know when *not* to laugh.

MICHAEL (*laughingly*) Yes, I expect that's it.

BOBBY (*to Gwen*) I like him.

GWEN. I don't.

(MICHAEL *laughs*)

BOBBY (*to Michael*) Look in at Lime Grove Studio this evening—about an hour's time—ask for me. I've got a television
show . . .

MICHAEL. Thanks a lot.

GWEN. Oh, no!

BOBBY. Damn it, the poor devil's got to live. I only want him
to report on my new song.

MICHAEL. I heard all the others. (*Moving to Gwen*) I thought
they were lousy.

(*He laughs out loud as* BOBBY *reacts—and* JOHN'S *voice is heard
from upstairs*)

JOHN (*off*) Well, let him get pneumonia! It'll do him good.
If he wears my overcoat, I'm through. Lock, stock and barrel,
I've finished with the whole damn thing!

(*A door is heard to slam.*
    GWEN *moves up and turns off the radiogram as* JOHN, *completely
out of control, hurriedly descends the stairs*)

GWEN. What's wrong, Daddy?

JOHN (*as he makes for the phone*) Don't speak to me. (*As he lifts
the receiver and dials*) I don't want *anybody* to speak to me!

BOBBY (*leaning against the piano*) It's going to be a very one-
sided phone conversation.

JOHN (*glaring at Bobby*) You mind your own damn business!
(*As he sees Michael*) And what the devil are you doing here? Get
out!

MICHAEL. Okay, sir. (*Laughing out loud as he turns to the windows*)
Here I go again! I'll be seeing you, Bobby.

(MICHAEL *exits through the french windows, as* JOHN *says*)

JOHN (*at the phone*) Hullo? . . . This is Mr John Bentley. I
want to speak to Mr Schneider.

BOBBY. Ah! Der wasser behälter mit de pull sing!

John (*at the phone*) Well, tell him to phone me. It's urgent.

(*He slams down the receiver as* Bobby *says*)

Bobby. Is there anything I can do, sir?
John (*moving* lc) Yes—you can go to hell!

(*He sits in the armchair* lc *and sinks his face into his hands as* Stella, *now wearing a fur cape with her evening dress, descends the stairs followed by* Peter. *He is still wearing his white beret and a black evening dress overcoat, borrowed from John's wardrobe, and is still wearing socks without shoes*)

Stella (*as she descends*) Bobby, you don't mind if Peter comes with us, do you?
Gwen. Oh, no!
Bobby (*moving* l) I don't think they'll let him in.
Stella (*moving* lc) He can sit with me. The only trouble is I can't find any shoes to fit him. (*To Peter*) You'll have to wear your brogues.

(Bobby *laughs out loud*)

Peter (*as he makes for the settee; smilingly, to Bobby*) I'll be the noisiest audience *you've* ever had.
Bobby (*laughing out loud*) I bet you stamp your feet.

(*He still laughs as* Peter *puts one brogue on, and as* Gwen *says*)

Gwen (*almost in tears; as she moves to Stella*) This is the meanest thing you've ever done to me!
Stella. Don't be selfish, Gwen. I can't leave him with your father.
Gwen (*tearfully as she leaves*) Come on, Bobby!

(Gwen *exits through the archway*)

Stella (*turning*) John, dear, do be sensible.
Gwen (*shouting angrily from off stage*) Bobby!
Bobby (*moving towards the archway*) Oh, all right!
Stella. Are you ready, Peter?

(Peter *stands at the* r *end of the settee with one foot half raised— and* Bobby, *at the archway, rocks with laughter*)

Peter. Yes, but—(*as he looks at the floor round about him*) I seem to be standing in something wet!
Bobby (*speaking with difficulty*) You're over-excited!

(*Rocking with laughter,* Bobby *exits through the archway, as* Peter *moves to follow him, still holding the other brogue in his hand*)

Peter (*loudly and suspiciously, as he follows Bobby*) Have you been putting anything *in* my brogues?

(*Peter exits through the archway, as* STELLA *moves to near her husband*)

STELLA. John—can't you understand? This is Gwen's *good-bye* to Bobby. It's a farewell to her first romance.

JOHN (*hoarsely, with a wild dramatic gesture*) Go away!

STELLA. Oh, very well. (*She moves up* C *then stops and looks back at John*) But, remember what Shakespeare said. (*She remembers playing Juliet, and she faces the audience as she continues*)

"Good night, good night, parting is such sweet sorrow,
    That we must say good night, 'til it be . . ."

(PETER *suddenly reappears in the archway, as he says loudly and petulantly*)

PETER (*to Stella*) Oh, come on, Mother!

(PETER *exits as* STELLA *freezes. Completely deflated, there is nothing for her to do but close her eyes and exit after Peter, in silence. The telephone rings.* JOHN *comes to life, springs to his feet, and moves up stage to grab the receiver*)

JOHN. Hullo? . . . Yes. Is that you, Schneider? . . . Good! Now listen! (*Slowly and emphatically*) What exactly did you mean when you suggested my bringing a strange woman here? . . . (*Loudly*) Well, *find* one for me! (*Loudly and desperately*) Yes—*as soon as possible!*

CURTAIN

ACT III

SCENE I

SCENE—*The same. About three hours later. Night.*
The windows are closed. The curtains have been half drawn to.
The lights are on. The low armchair, from LC, *has been moved into and*
against the "waist" of the piano. LC *there is a "waiter" carrying a*
couple of opened champagne bottles and an empty glass. At R *of the*
"waiter" is a small chair. There are two or three empty glasses on the
downstage end of the piano. On the long table behind the settee are two
opened champagne bottles, a half full bottle of brandy, and several
glasses. Peter's brown-paper parcel is on the R *end of the drinks table.*

Before the CURTAIN *rises the radiogram can be heard playing, and voices*
singing the end of one of the verses of a record of "Down Yonder".

When the CURTAIN *rises* JOHN *is sitting at the* L *end of the settee. He is*
wearing Peter's white beret, a dressing-gown, and a flowery scarf. His
arm is round PEARL'S *waist. Her head is on his shoulder. He holds an*
empty glass. PEARL *is about twenty-four, a platinum blonde, and quite*
beautiful. She wears a sleek black evening frock, with a slim wrapped
coat of claret velvet, and rhinestone ear-rings. SCHNEIDER *is sitting in*
the chair R *of the "waiter". He wears a shabby dinner jacket—he's*
smoking a cigar and holding a glass of whisky. PETER, *still in the blue*
shorts, etc., is sitting on the piano, with his feet on the back of the small
armchair. He is clumsily trying to knit a fantastically coloured scarf.
JOHN, PETER *and* SCHNEIDER *slightly advertise the fact that they*
have had more than enough to drink. PEARL *is cold sober, but the*
adverb is metaphorical. All present launch into the chorus with gusto.
At the end of the Chorus, there is a general cheer and—if it hasn't
*already done so automatically—*SCHNEIDER *switches off the radiogram.*
SCHNEIDER. Bravo!

PETER (*at the top of his voice*) Bentley for Chairman!
JOHN (*rising and moving the microphone to* C) I am now going to
sing a little song, all by myself.
PETER (*getting down from the piano*) Oh, no, you're not!
JOHN. Oh, yes, I am! If Bobby Denver can croon—anybody
can croon.
SCHNEIDER (*moving to sit at the piano*) I vill play for you—vot
is it to be?
JOHN. Something my office boy has been singing for the past
six months—and has it made me cry!
PETER (*crossing behind John to sit on the* L *end of the settee*) Hit it,
Hermann!

55

(JOHN *switches on the microphone.* SCHNEIDER *plays and* JOHN *sings "Cry"—in serious burlesque—directly to the audience. At the conclusion,* PETER, SCHNEIDER *and* PEARL *applaud and cheer—and* PETER *rises and takes the microphone back to near the piano keyboard, clearing the flex as he does so, as* PEARL *says*)

PEARL (*to John*) Darling, you sing like a nightingale.
JOHN (*mopping his forehead*) Thank you, darling.
PEARL. I can sing too.
JOHN (*moving* RC) Really? Who taught you?
SCHNEIDER (*rising and moving* C) I did. She occupies a little flat next to my own. Each night, I give 'er a lesson qvite free.
PETER (*to Schneider*) Well, I think you should *pay*. (*He crosses behind Schneider to above the settee*)
JOHN (*at the* L *end of settee; to Pearl*) What is your name again, darling?
PEARL. Pearl.
JOHN. Charming. And is Schneider your oyster?
PEARL. I don't know what you mean. (*Holding out her arms*) Give me a little kiss.
JOHN (*indicating Peter and Schneider*) Not in front of the children.
SCHNEIDER (*laughingly*) Ve can go into ze garden.
PETER (*continuing his knitting; moving below the* R *end of the settee*) Not for me. I enjoy nothing more than watching an elderly man make a clot of himself.
PEARL (*to John*) Why don't you throw him out?
JOHN. Because I don't want anybody to know he's been here. (*Crossing to Peter*) But later, I shall find myself a pair of scissors and remove his whiskers!
PETER (*grinning, as he continues to knit*) You resent my beard, don't you? It's a threat to the common level of your green meadow gregariousness. You ridicule it because it offends your bovine mediocrity.
JOHN. Peter, darling, you slay me.

(*With a little dance step,* JOHN *moves up to the drinks table to refill his glass*)

SCHNEIDER (*to Peter*) Vy don't you be'ave yourself? You 'ave already been kicked out from television. If you are not careful, ze same sing vill 'appen here.
PETER. Oh, no. Be it ever so humble, this is my home—and an Englishman's home is his schlosh.
PEARL. There's no need to use disgusting words. Can't you talk seriously for a change?
PETER. But of course. (*He sits on the settee* R *of Pearl and leans his head on Pearl's shoulder, as he continues. Over-seriously*) Tell me, my darling, what do you think of the hereafter?
SCHNEIDER. Ah, no! No politics!

(JOHN *drains his refilled glass, as* PETER *says*)

PETER (*resignedly; as he rises*) Oh, very well. I shall go into the kitchen and make a pass at Linda.

SCHNEIDER (*irritably*) She is preparing sandwiches.

PETER (*making for the archway*) Good! I can take her unawares. (*Turning, as he smiles wickedly*) If you hear anybody screaming, it'll be *me*.

(PETER *exits, with his knitting, as* SCHNEIDER *says*)

SCHNEIDER (*following Peter*) Damn lunatic! Vy don't you mind your own business!

(SCHNEIDER *exits through the archway*)

PEARL (*sweetly*) Mr Bentley.

JOHN (*putting down his glass*) What is it, darling?

PEARL. This isn't quite the set-up I expected.

JOHN (*moving to the settee*) How do you mean?

PEARL. Well, you're not very interested in me, are you? After all, I consider myself fairly attractive—and I'm not used to spending *platonic* evenings with strange men. I think you've been most insulting.

JOHN (*sitting* L *of Pearl*) Didn't Schneider explain that I had no—er—requirements?

PEARL. Yes—but can't you change your mind?

JOHN. My dear girl, we're discussing a standard of behaviour. We're not backing horses.

PEARL (*petulantly*) You got me here under false pretences.

JOHN. I did nothing of the sort. It was a strictly non-biological business arrangement which you understood perfectly well. Our relationship is no more than that of a managing director and his private secretary.

PEARL. Oh, sir! (*Jumping on to his lap*) Just one little kiss!

JOHN (*putting her back on to the settee*) Absolutely, no.

PEARL (*petulantly*) Don't you ever want to kiss your *real* secretary?

JOHN. Not with any overpowering inclination. He's a middle-aged Scotsman with five children.

PEARL (*laughingly, as she puts her arms round him*) Now you're being silly.

JOHN (*removing her arms*) Pearl, darling, please remember— you're *Schneider's* trophy, not mine.

(JOHN *rises and moves to* C)

PEARL. All right, Mr Bentley—·I shall want another ten pounds for wasting my time like this. If you don't give it to me, I shall make things difficult for you.

JOHN. How?

PEARL (*rising and moving to him*)   I shall tell your wife there has been nothing between us.

JOHN (*aghast*)   You wouldn't do that?

PEARL (*putting her arms round his shoulders*)   Oh, yes, I would.

(SCHNEIDER *enters through the archway*)

SCHNEIDER (*continuing down to* LC)   Ah-ha!

JOHN (*to Schneider*)   Listen! Have you been teaching her the psychological approach to business?

SCHNEIDER.   Only ze first lesson.

JOHN.   Well, cut it out. She's matriculated.

(PEARL *sits on the* L *arm of the settee, as* PETER *hurries in through the archway and shouts*)

PETER.   Where's my parcel? (*As he sees it and takes it up*)   Ah!

JOHN.   What have you *got* there?

PETER (*clutching the parcel to his chest*)   The preliminary model of my masterpiece in sculpture!

JOHN.   I thought you were a playwright.

PETER.   Damn it, can't I have a hobby? I'm going to give it to Linda. I find her completely unresponsive. It will awaken her to the naked facts of life!

JOHN (*grabbing the parcel from Peter*)   Give me that!

(SCHNEIDER *hurriedly moves the bottles from the "waiter" to the drinks table, and* JOHN *puts the parcel on the "waiter" and rips off the string*)

PETER.   Well, be careful!

(JOHN *throws aside the brown paper, and holds up a shapeless lump of "clay"—plasticine—about the size of a football. It has a large hole through its middle*)

JOHN.   What the hell is it?

PETER.   It's a horse.

(JOHN *looks at Peter, then drops the "clay" on to the "waiter" and stares at it*)

JOHN (*to Peter*)   Which part of the horse?

PETER (*holding his forehead*)   It's the whole horse!

JOHN.   But it hasn't got any legs.

PETER.   It did have—but I removed them. When an artist finds that his work is beginning to resemble something, he should stop.

JOHN.   I don't think he should begin. What's its name?

PETER.   Rebecca.

JOHN.   Oh. It's a mare?

PETER.   No, no! Sex doesn't enter into this at all.

JOHN.   I'm not surprised. (*To Schneider, as he indicates the shapeless "clay"*)   Is this art?

SCHNEIDER (*moving to* L *of John*) But certainly. Rodin said zat sculpture is nossing more zan a lump. Vot matters is 'ow you *look* at ze lumps!

JOHN. Right! (*As he slaps the "clay"*) This is mine.

PETER. Oh, no!

JOHN (*turning up his cuffs*) From now on, I am *an artist*—with all the right to be Bohemian, immoral and unwashed. (*He pounds at the "clay" with his fist*)

PETER (*in agony*) Aaaah! You damn vandal! God will punish you for this! I can't stand it! (*Turning and making for the stairs*) He's ruined it! (*He ascends the stairs, as he continues. Brokenly*) He's ruined my horse!

(PETER *exits*)

JOHN (*briskly*) Pearl—for an additional five pounds, you will adopt a piquant pose on the piano.

PEARL (*rising*) In the nude?

JOHN. Certainly.

(PEARL *crosses to the piano as she removes her claret coat*)

PEARL (*very happy*) Oh, good! This is going to be fun.

SCHNEIDER. Mr Bentleys, for in ze nude—zere is not enough clay. I speak from experience.

JOHN (*still working the "clay"*) Oh, very well. I'll do a mask. (*To Pearl*) Just the face, darling.

PEARL (*angrily, to Schneider*) Why the hell did *you* have to interfere?

SCHNEIDER. You can still pose on ze piano. You 'ave got nice legs.

(PEARL *steps on to the small armchair and sits on the piano, showing her nice legs as she says*)

PEARL (*to Schneider*) You make me sick!

JOHN (*to Pearl*) That's the expression I want. (*As he works furiously on the "clay"*) Steady now—hold it!

(GWEN, *still in evening dress, hurries in through the archway*)

GWEN (*as she enters*) They're half killing Bobby. He's ... (*She stops, then continues*) What does this mean?

JOHN (*to Pearl*) Don't move, darling.

GWEN (*livid; to John*) *What* did you call her?

JOHN (*very busy*) It was only a theatrical expression. It doesn't mean anything.

GWEN (*moving up* C) You've been drinking. Oh, Daddy! You're not going to let Stella see you like this?

JOHN. Why not? You've all been having fun. Now it's my turn. I'm very grateful to you, Gwen. Your own carefree outlook on life has opened up a whole new world to me. No more worrying about the future. No more responsibility or sense of duty. I'm in love with my new freedom—and the family can go to blazes!

GWEN (*wildly; to John*) Stella will divorce you for this!

JOHN. That's okay by me. (*Indicating Pearl*) I'll marry Pearl.

GWEN. *What!*

PEARL (*to John*) Oh, darling! I'd love that!

JOHN (*to Pearl*) How old are you, my sweet?

PEARL. Twenty-four.

GWEN (*to John; tearfully*) You're forty-six!

JOHN. That's nothing! John Knox was a hundred and fifty-nine when he fell in love with Rose la Touche. And if you marry Bobby Denver, his new stepmother-in-law will be thirteen years younger than he is. *That'll* make him feel pretty ancient, won't it?

GWEN (*wildly*) I'm ashamed of you! (*Tearfully*) You're a wicked man!

JOHN. Maybe I am. But I've never threatened to hit *my* father.

GWEN (*wildly*) If she stays here, I'll kill her!

PEARL (*to Gwen*) I think you're being awfully silly.

GWEN (*wildly; to Pearl*) Don't speak to me! (*Tearfully she turns and makes for the french windows*) I won't stay in the same house with you! (*Glaring back at Pearl*) You common concubine!

(GWEN *bursts into tears, turns, flings open one of the french windows and exits into the garden, as* SCHNEIDER *crosses down* R)

PEARL (*to John*) Was she hinting at something?

SCHNEIDER (*irritably*) Don't be so sensitive.

(BOBBY, *still in evening dress, comes hurrying in through the archway*)

BOBBY (*moving* RC) Good Lord! What goes on?

(JOHN *models furiously without looking up*)

SCHNEIDER (*to Bobby*) Ssh!

PEARL (*smilingly as she slips the top of her frock from her shoulders*) Hullo, Bobby Denver!

BOBBY (*moving to her*) Hullo, darling. (*Having kissed her on the lips*) Who are *you?*

SCHNEIDER. She is a model for Mr Bentleys. Plis don't disturb 'im.

BOBBY. Has he gone cuckoo?

SCHNEIDER. 'E 'as found 'is vocation.

BOBBY. I didn't know he'd lost it.

(MICHAEL *enters through the archway, takes one look at John's white beret, and bursts out laughing*)

SCHNEIDER (*angrily*) Ssh!

MICHAEL (*to Bobby*) Has Gwen seen this?

BOBBY. I don't know. (*To Schneider*) Where is she?

SCHNEIDER. In ze garden. She vos a little upset.

BOBBY. I'm not surprised. (*To Michael*) Go and look after her, will you?

MICHAEL. Okay.

(MICHAEL *has another glance at John, laughs out loud, and exits into the garden*)

JOHN (*loudly and petulantly as he slaps down a lump of "clay"*) I find it quite impossible to work with all this noise going on!

BOBBY. I'm sorry. I didn't know you'd started.

JOHN (*indignantly*) Started? I've nearly finished.

BOBBY (*looking at the lump of "clay"*) Well, there's one thing about it—it isn't rude.

JOHN (*staring at Pearl*) If only I can get those eyes! Wait now! Don't move!

(*With outstretched fingers,* JOHN *excitedly measures Pearl's eyes, as* STELLA, *still in evening dress, enters through the archway*)

STELLA (*angrily*) What does this mean?

JOHN (*over his shoulder*) Stand back! Oh! Hullo, darling. Excuse me a moment.

(JOHN *hurriedly has one more check of the eye measurement, then —with his two fingers raised in the air, he hurries back to above the "waiter". Slowly he draws back his hand, then lunges his fingers into the "clay". Slowly and tensely, he withdraws them and anxiously leans forward to study the result*)

(*Excitedly*) Oh, wonderful! Denver—what do you think of it?

BOBBY (*moving to* L *of John*) Magnificent! (*Crossing behind John to up* RC; *to Stella*) Imagine what he could do with a bit of wire!

(PEARL *gets down from the piano and moves to* JOHN *and he smilingly puts an arm round her and hugs her to him—as* STELLA *moves to* R *of the "waiter"*)

STELLA (*as she looks at the "clay"*) Oh, yes! It's quite something, isn't it? One can almost see the Edgware Road. (*Charmingly, to Pearl*) My husband must know you quite well.

PEARL (*with charm and emphasis*) Intimately.

STELLA (*surprised*) Really? I don't know which of you to congratulate. (*Indicating the "clay"*) This *is* supposed to be your face, isn't it?

PEARL} (*together*) Of course.
JOHN }

STELLA (*as she turns and grabs a champagne bottle—a wooden replica—from the drinks table just behind her*) Good!

(STELLA *viciously wallops the "clay" with the bottle—and leaves it clinging to the "clay", as* PEARL *hurriedly leaves John, grabs her coat from the piano, crosses to Schneider as she gasps*)

c

PEARL (*as she goes*) For Pete's sake!

(STELLA *has already grabbed a loose piece of "clay" and, moving down* C, *she flings it at* PEARL, *as she almost screams*)

STELLA. Get out! Get out before I tear you to pieces!

(SCHNEIDER, *babbling a torrent of ad lib. German, grabs* PEARL, *and together they panic away through the archway, as* JOHN *says*)

JOHN (*to Stella*) Control yourself! Don't you realize that, at any moment, the earth may lose its atmosphere?

STELLA (*tearfully*) I'll never forgive you for this. Never!

(JOHN *pushes the "waiter" away to up* L *and moves down* C *to* L *of Stella, as he says*)

JOHN (*emphatically*) To coin a phrase, I couldn't care less! I've had a little fling and I've thoroughly enjoyed myself. But I'm not going to settle down and lose my personality. I'm going to go on having little flings. This was only a rehearsal.

(*A high-pitched whine comes from* STELLA, *as she presses her handkerchief to her mouth*)

BOBBY (*moving down to* R *of Stella*) Pull yourself together. He was only putting on an act.

STELLA (*sobbingly, to Bobby*) Every wife knows it must happen sooner or later—but for a man to be unfaithful, just out of spite . . .

BOBBY. He hasn't been unfaithful. (*To John*) Have you?

JOHN (*smilingly*) Only metaphorically.

STELLA. There, you see? He's admitted it! (*Brokenly, to John*) All the rest of my life now, I shall see the shadow of a woman tip-toeing behind you! (*Wildly*) I don't want to live! (*As she makes for the stairs*) I don't want to live!

BOBBY. What are you going to do?

STELLA (*dramatically as she looks back from the foot of the stairs*) That doesn't matter much. What *does* matter—is how I do it! (*Remembering her last performance at the "Haymarket," she slowly and magnificently ascends the stairs as she continues. With high tragedy*) And I'm going to do it—beautifully!

(STELLA *magnificently exits*)

BOBBY. Oh, Lord, what does that remind me of? It was in a play somewhere. (*As he thinks hard*) "I'm going to do it beauti-fully. Do it beautifully." (*Suddenly*) Bentley! It was *Hedda Gabler!* She's going to shoot herself!

JOHN (*calmly, as he smiles*) Upstairs? All alone? Without an audience? It would be a physical impossibility. Why, even when she played *The Second Mrs Tanqueray*, she couldn't bring herself to die off stage. They had to re-write the end of the play.

(PETER *frantically half-way descends the stairs, as he gasps*)

PETER. Stella! She's in the bathroom! Writhing on the floor! She's foaming at the mouth! Quickly!

(PETER *tears back up the stairs, frantically followed by* JOHN)

JOHN (*as he ascends the stairs; to Bobby*)   Phone the doctor!
BOBBY. What's the number?
JOHN. I don't know—phone and ask him!

(JOHN *exits up the stairs after Peter, as* LINDA *comes hurrying in through the archway*)

LINDA (*immediately, urgently and anxiously*)   Is anything wrong, sir?
BOBBY (*immediately and urgently, as he moves to her*)   Linda, this is serious! What's the doctor's phone number?
LINDA (*flustered*)   Er—er—er . . .

(BOBBY *takes her by the elbows, his face close to hers*)

BOBBY. The number! Quickly!
LINDA (*flustered*)   I can't remember it, sir—not when you look at me so close!
BOBBY (*shaking her, and raising his voice angrily*)   Damn it, pull yourself together! What's the number?
LINDA (*breaking down*)   Oh, don't be cross with me, Bobby! (*Loudly and tearfully*) I couldn't bear you to be cross with me!
BOBBY (*immediately, and with gentle and soothing charm*)   Linda, darling, I'm not cross with you. (*As though to a child*) Bobby only wants to know the number. Bobby likes you. Bobby almost *loves* you.

(LINDA *closes her eyes and moans.* BOBBY *mechanically moves to behind her, and as she passes out backwards, he catches her. Silently and mechanically, he exits backwards through the archway and* LINDA, *still unconscious, exits with him—as* PETER *slowly descends the stairs to sit mopingly at the foot of them. One second—and* BOBBY *comes hurrying back through the archway*)

(*Immediately; to Peter*) Is she still alive? (*He moves* C)

(PETER *nods*)

Then why are you looking so miserable?
PETER (*as he rises and leaves the stairs and moves to* LC)   I'm pondering the Stygian chicanery of women. Do you know what caused that awful frothing at the mouth?
BOBBY. No.
PETER. Half a tube of my toothpaste.
BOBBY. Are you sure?
PETER (*showing the tube*)   I took it out of her hand as we got her on to the bed—and she opened one eye and whispered, "Don't say anything!"
BOBBY. Did you tell Bentley?
C*

PETER. No. He'd fallen on his knees and was deep in prayer. I didn't like to interrupt him.

BOBBY (*as he makes for the stairs*) My God, you're as mad as they are!

(BOBBY *hurriedly exits up the stairs as* PAT, *still in evening dress, enters through the archway.* PETER *at* LC *remains motionless for a moment as he stares at her, then murmurs*)

PETER. Oh, Pat.

PAT (*moving* C) What's the matter? Do I look too unspecified, too ordinary? Have I joined the common throng? Have I let you down?

(PETER *is silent for a moment. He glances at his blue shorts and yellow brogues*)

PETER. I feel rather ridiculous.

PAT (*surprised*) You mean you're not fed up with me for dressing like this?

PETER (*smiling as he shakes his head*) No. You look . . . (*Pause*) I've never seen anything like it!

PAT. Was it going to be something complimentary?

PETER. Much more than that.

PAT. But I don't understand. Have you lost your faith, or been converted?

PETER. I was going to ask *you* that.

PAT. All right. I'll give you the answer. (*Steadily*) I'm never going back to the Boulevard St Germain—and I never again want to hear the word Existentialist. I'm going to live an ordinary normal life, with ordinary normal people, and if you find that impossible—(*her voice breaking*) well, it's just too bad.

PETER. Now may I tell *you* something?

PAT. Go ahead.

PETER (*steadily*) I've hated almost every moment of our life in Paris. I don't really know what the word Existentialist means, and I know absolutely nothing about sculpture. (*Loudly and irritably*) I feel frozen to death in these damn shorts, I hate this beard—and I've always wanted to live near Wimbledon Common.

PAT. Peter!

(*She puts her arms out to him and he moves to her and holds her close. She looks up at him*)

(*Really very puzzled*) But why on earth have you been behaving like a crazy lunatic all these weeks?

PETER. You forget what you were like when we first met. You were screamingly bored by anything commonplace—you jeered at everything conventional. Picasso was your patron saint—James Joyce your Bible. You swore like a trooper, you drank your whisky neat—and it was only with the greatest difficulty I stopped you chewing tobacco.

PAT. But that was only a phase. It was a revulsion against
Father.

PETER. Maybe, but *I* didn't know that—and I thought that if
I didn't act crazy too, I'd lose you. (*Pause, then quietly*) And I
didn't *want* to lose you.

(*She looks up at him and he kisses her on the lips—then continues*)

So I didn't tell you I was writing a play about Queen Victoria—
and I didn't tell you . . . (*He pauses and looks worried*)

PAT. What?

PETER (*quietly, as he turns away*) I don't think I can.

PAT. But you must! Is it anything dreadful?

PETER. *I* don't think so—but *you* might.

PAT. Anything to do with a woman?

PETER (*unhappily*) No.

PAT. Oh, Peter, tell me! I understand most things about life—
and I'm tremendously forgiving.

PETER (*reluctantly*) All right. (*He looks at her*) Pat—I'm a
Conservative.

(*They laugh together. He moves to her and takes her hands*)

Shall I tell you something else?

PAT. Yes.

PETER (*smilingly*) I'm hungry.

PAT (*laughingly, as she moves to the archway*) I'll get you a
sandwich.

(PETER *moves to her, and she stops as he says*)

PETER. Darling, the kitchen's full of them. Linda's prepared a
whole banquet. (*Quietly*) I love you so much.

(BOBBY *appears at the head of the stairs and quietly descends them,
as* PETER *continues*)

(*To Pat*) I wish I could tell you how you looked when you came
into the room just now.

PAT. Well, try. Did I look pretty?

PETER. Oh, yes.

(BOBBY *switches on his microphone and quietly sits at the piano, as*
PETER *continues*)

But that doesn't describe it. You looked—you looked . . .

BOBBY (*playing quietly and singing sincerely without tears*)
            Sweet and lovely . . .

PETER (*to Pat; quietly*) That's it!

(PAT *puts her arms round Peter.* BOBBY *has continued singing*)

BOBBY.   Sweeter than the roses in May—

(PETER *kisses* PAT **on** *the lips.* BOBBY *has continued*)

BOBBY.   And she loves me—

(PETER *holds* PAT *close to him as they move to the archway.*
BOBBY *has continued*)

Heaven must have sent her my way.
Skies above me—
Never were as blue as her eyes—

(PETER *and* PAT *exit together as* BOBBY *continues*)

And she loves me—
Who could want a sweeter surprise . . .

(GWEN, *angry and desperate, enters through the french windows and
makes for the stairs.* BOBBY *switches off the microphone, as he says*)
Where are *you* going?

GWEN (*pausing up* LC) Upstairs—to pack. I won't stay here
another night!

BOBBY (*rising*) You know, if you go on like this you'll be sent
to one of those schools.

(MICHAEL *smilingly enters through the french windows as* GWEN
replies)

GWEN (*her eyes narrowing*) Oh, no! Nobody's going to send me
anywhere! I'm going to follow you for the rest of my life. When
you stay at the Savoy, I shall live in an attic nearby. If you go to
America, I shall stow away on the same ship. If you rejoin your
wife, I shall separate you. When you become old and ill, I shall
look after you. And when you die—I shall die, too.

MICHAEL. Never underestimate the power of a woman.

GWEN (*moving* C; *to Michael*) Oh, shut up!

BOBBY (*quietly*) Michael.

MICHAEL. Yes?

BOBBY. Would you mind?

MICHAEL. You mean, out again?

BOBBY. Just for a few moments.

MICHAEL. Sure. I've had quite a long stay, for me.

(MICHAEL *laughingly exits through the french windows.* BOBBY
looks at Gwen)

BOBBY. I didn't expect *you* to break a promise.

GWEN. How do you mean?

BOBBY. You swore on your oath that if we spent the evening
together you'd stop all this nonsense.

GWEN. We weren't *alone* together. Anyway, if I *did* swear on
my oath I can't keep to it. (*Moving to him*) Bobby, is it because
I'm only sixteen that you won't take any notice of me?

BOBBY. That's one reason, yes.

GWEN. What's the other?

BOBBY. I'm *over* sixteen.

GWEN. If you were twenty, and I were nineteen—would you take any notice of me then?

BOBBY. Oh, yes, rather.

GWEN. Well, can't you *pretend* I'm nineteen?

BOBBY. Yes, but I can't pretend I'm twenty.

GWEN (*serious and adoring*) I was quite close to you tonight when you were singing—and I saw the tears streaming down your face. Only in you have I found somebody tremblingly alive to all the sorrow in the world. Somebody who can't even whisper the words "Good-bye" or "Forgive me" without his eyes filling with tears. It was like finding water in the desert. And now—(*her voice breaking*) away from you, I couldn't live.

BOBBY. You're not in love with *me*. You're in love with tragedy. You've been reading too much Dusty-Dosty-what's-his-name. You'll make quite a writer yourself when you grow up a bit and get a sense of proportion. At the moment you're just wallowing in sloppy sentiment.

GWEN (*shocked*) This isn't you speaking.

BOBBY. It certainly is. And I've got another surprise for you. I haven't cried real tears since I was a kid. I've never been able to *see* the tragic side of life, and I've never found anything to cry *about*. I'm a comic! Until recently I was perfectly happy making people laugh. All this weeping warbler stuff is giving me the willies!

GWEN. You mean your tears weren't real this evening?

BOBBY. No.

GWEN. Were they real that Monday at the *Coliseum*?

BOBBY. No.

GWEN (*desperately*) Oh, Bobby, I don't believe you! You're trying to keep me away from you. Tell me it isn't true. If you don't, I'll kill myself! (*Tearfully but insistently*) They *are* real, aren't they?

BOBBY. No, they're not! I can't cry at all. I use an onion.

(*A pause.* GWEN *stares at him*)

GWEN (*in a whisper*) You're fooling.

BOBBY. I'm not. (*Producing a small onion from his trouser pocket*) This is the one I used to break your father up. "High Noon"— remember? And I used it again tonight. At the right moment I stick my finger into it, touch my eyelids—and it's a physical impossibility to whisper "Good-bye", "Forgive me"—or even "Bob's your uncle", without the tears simply *streaming* down!

(*He puts the onion back in his pocket as* GWEN *half turns away, bends her head, and presses a hand to her face*)

Oh, come on, Gwen! Be a man. You've got to face *up* to life.

GWEN (*brokenly, in a whisper*) Don't speak to me!

BOBBY (*gently as he moves to her*) Listen . . .

GWEN (*wildly, as she makes for the archway*) Go away!

(GWEN *exits*)

BOBBY (*moving* RC) Poor silly damn kid—why did she have to pick on me? (*At the top of his voice*) Michael!

(MICHAEL *hurries in through the french windows*)

That was very quick.

MICHAEL (*as he makes for the archway*) She's going to take some looking after *this* time.

BOBBY. Were you listening?

MICHAEL (*laughingly*) Of course!

(MICHAEL *hurriedly exits through the archway—and* JOHN—*without beret—enters to descend the stairs, slowly—as* BOBBY *takes his handkerchief and dabs one eye. He looks at the handkerchief*)

BOBBY. Good Lord! It's a real one. A *real* tear! (*As he carefully folds the handkerchief so as not to crease the tear*) Oh, if only I could have it stuffed.

JOHN (*dully as he leaves the stairs and moves to* LC) I can remember when that sort of conversation would have sounded quite strange.

BOBBY (*replacing the handkerchief into his breast pocket*) How's Stella?

JOHN. The toothpaste upset her stomach. She's feeling very weak. She has only just enough strength to prop herself up and whisper the most poisonous remarks about my mother.

BOBBY. I told her you hadn't been unfaithful.

JOHN. So did I. But we're just two little sparrows beating our wings against a wall of feminine granite. If I live to be a hundred and ninety, I shall spend every remaining hour of my life under the shadow of guilt and suspicion. (*Moving to him*) Bobby—you'll have to stay the night here.

BOBBY. I can't.

JOHN. My dear old friend, you must. Any moment now—and she'll rise from her bed of sickness to begin my cross-examination. I can't go through it by myself!

(LINDA *enters through the archway, carrying a large silver tray, with coffee-pot, milk jug, four cups and saucers, four small plates, four knives—and two large plates piled high with sandwiches. She reaches the foot of the stairs, and* JOHN *half turns, as he says*)

Er—Linda.

LINDA (*turning and moving down* L) Yes, sir?

JOHN. Prepare the little bedroom next to yours, will you?

LINDA (*still holding the over-loaded tray*) Very good, sir. Who's going to occupy it, sir?

John (*indicating*) Mr Denver.

(*A violent tremor shakes* Linda *from head to foot. She moans, closes her eyes, and staggers backwards as she clenches her teeth in an effort to retain consciousness, as* John *shouts*)

Put the tray down!

Bobby (*to Linda*) Put your head between your knees!

With a mighty effort, Linda *digs her heels into the carpet and stands still for half a second. Then with another moan and increasing speed she totters sideways across the room towards* John *and* Bobby. *With cries of dismay, they fling themselves through the open french windows, and* Linda *follows, almost on top of them. A second's pause, a terrific crash, and shouts from the garden are heard as—*

the Curtain *falls*

Scene 2

Scene—*The same. The following morning. About* 9 *a.m.*
    All evidence of the previous night's party has been tidied away. On a chair at the R *side of the drinks table there is an overcoat and a hat. The french windows are closed, the curtains open.*

When the Curtain *rises,* John *is discovered, full length on the settee and fast asleep. He is covered by a blanket, and his head rests on a cushion. He is dressed as for the previous scene. His hair is ruffled. A moment, and the telephone rings.* John *mumbles, without moving.*

John. Hullo. Hullo! (*He opens his eyes, groans and props himself up. Holding his head*) Phew! (*Suddenly he realizes that the phone is ringing, and still half asleep and with a hang-over he rises and staggers to the phone, trailing and tripping over the blanket. Hoarsely, having lifted the receiver*) Hullo? . . . Hold on. (*He rests the receiver, moves to the stairs and shouts upwards*) Bentley! (*He suddenly "does a take", hurries back to the phone, lifts the receiver and says*) Speaking.

(Linda *enters with a cup of tea, as* John *continues*)

Who? . . . Michael Kenley? . . . (*Immediately brisk and alert*) Is Gwen still with you? Good! . . . Yes, get a taxi at once . . . Good-bye.

(John *replaces the receiver as* Linda *asks*)

Linda (*as she puts the tea on the settee table*) Is she all right, sir?
John (*holding out the blanket to Linda*) Yes. She'll be here in a few minutes.
Linda (*taking the blanket*) Is she still with that reporter?

JOHN (*taking up the cup of tea*)   Mind your own business. What's the time?

LINDA.   Nine o'clock, sir.

JOHN (*pointing*)   Whose overcoat?

(JOHN *sips his tea, and moves* L *as* LINDA *replies*)

LINDA (*as she folds up the blanket*)   Mr Denver's, sir. A chauffeur brought it from the Savoy Hotel. I didn't like to take it up to his bedroom.

JOHN.   Is Mrs Bentley up?

LINDA (*moving* C)   Oh, yes, sir. She went out nearly an hour ago.

JOHN.   Did she look as though she might be going for good?

LINDA.   How do you mean, sir?

JOHN.   Well, did she take her mink coat with her?

LINDA.   Oh, no, sir.

JOHN.   She'll be back.

LINDA (*moving towards the stairs, with the blanket*)   Will you be sleeping upstairs tonight, sir?

JOHN (*holding his head*)   I hope not! For the rest of my life I shall regard that bedroom as the headquarters of the Spanish Inquisition.

LINDA (*unhappily*)   Very good, sir.

(LINDA *exits up the stairs, and* JOHN *turns to find that* STELLA *has entered to the archway. She is dressed for out-of-doors*)

STELLA (*with a charming smile*)   Good morning.

(JOHN, *at* LC, *remains silently staring at her.* STELLA *moves to him. She kisses him on the cheek*)

JOHN (*surprised*)   Oh, no! This isn't true! I'm delirious!

STELLA.   You deserve to be. Any news of Gwen?

JOHN.   Yes. Michael's just phoned. They were at Baker Street. He was just getting a taxi.

STELLA.   Thank heaven for that.

JOHN.   Where have *you* been?

(STELLA *removes her hat and places it on the settee table, as she replies*)

STELLA.   Visiting your pseudo *fille de joie*.

JOHN (*moving* C)   Do you mean Pearl?

STELLA.   Of course.

JOHN.   You actually called on her?

STELLA (*moving to* R *of John*)   Certainly. I knocked three times and she opened the door at once. We had a cup of tea, and a little chat, and parted most amicably.

JOHN.   Did she explain?

STELLA.   Everything.

JOHN (*amazed*) And you believed her?

STELLA. Absolutely.

(JOHN *puts a hand to his forehead, and crosses to sit on the settee*)

What's the matter?

JOHN. For six hours last night I swore on my oath and on my knees, and you wouldn't believe a word I said. This morning, you have a cup of tea and a little chat with a comparatively complete stranger and you accept the same explanation *lock, stock* and *barrel*.

STELLA (*moving to sit L of him*) This morning I *knew* I was being told the truth. No woman can successfully lie to another woman. Over a cup of tea we instinctively see through each other. (*Taking his hand*) I think we can be happy again.

JOHN. I hope so. I'll try and make life a bit brighter for you. Take you to theatres and night clubs. We'll start tonight!

STELLA. Oh, no, we won't! When I looked at myself in the mirror this morning I thought I looked tired and ugly. (*Pause*) I said I thought I looked tired and ugly.

JOHN (*meekly*) I'm not arguing, dear.

(LINDA *enters to descend the stairs*)

LINDA (*as she sees Stella*) Oh, thank heaven you've come back, ma'am. (*As she makes for the archway*) Mr Bentley was trying to work out whether you might have gone for good.

(LINDA *exits as* STELLA *gives John an old-fashioned look*)

JOHN (*forcing a laugh*) She put that very badly.

STELLA. Yes. Now, you have a shave and pull yourself together!

(JOHN *rises and moves towards the stairs*)

And when Gwen arrives for heaven's sake behave as though nothing had happened.

JOHN. You mean I'm not to question her about walking round London all night?

STELLA. Of course not! (*Rising and moving to near the french windows*) She was with Michael, and he phoned us at least six times to tell us she was all right.

JOHN (*moving C*) Why didn't he bring her home? Why didn't he tell us where we could find her?

STELLA (*moving to the R end of the settee*) She wanted to be alone. Can't you understand that there are moments in even a child's life when the words father and mother make her want to scream?

JOHN (*as he moves to the L end of the settee*) My God, Shakespeare knew what he was doing when he wrote "Blow, blow"—whatever it was. And I ought to know better than to be upset by it. (*Moving to L of Stella*) The only way to raise children is to have at least seventeen, give them all numbers, and as soon as they've attained the age of reason—throw them out!

(LINDA *hurries in through the archway with a newspaper*)

LINDA (*as she enters*) Oh, sir! Look at this! (*Moving to* L *of John*) It's all about Miss Gwen and Bobby Denver!

(JOHN *takes the newspaper*)

STELLA (*to Linda*) What d'you mean?

LINDA. He's phoney, ma'am!

STELLA (*to John*) What does it say?

JOHN (*quoting*) "Struggle on Embankment. Famous crooner mentioned. Late last night, near Chelsea Bridge, Police Constable Riley went to the assistance of a man struggling with a young girl who appeared to be trying to throw herself into the Thames. When questioned, the girl, who seemed quite heartbroken, sobbingly assured Constable Riley that the tears of Bobby Denver, the well-known crying crooner, were produced with the aid of an onion. Enquiries at the Savoy Hotel elicited no reply from Mr Denver. He was not at home."

STELLA (*moving* R *above the settee table*) Thank God it doesn't mention *her* name.

JOHN (*unbelievingly*) She tried to throw herself into the Thames?

STELLA. It doesn't *say* that. It says she *appeared* to be trying. And knowing Gwen, I'm quite sure she'd already made certain that the tide was out.

JOHN (*moving to* L *of Stella*) This'll finish Denver.

LINDA (*tearfully*) And so it should!

STELLA. Get on with your work, Linda. It's nothing to do with you.

LINDA (*tearfully*) Oh, yes, it is! He's broken *my* heart as well as hers. I've never fallen for *any* man as often as I've fallen for him!

(*Sobbing freely*, LINDA *turns towards the archway and happens to see* BOBBY *as he enters to descend the stairs—still in evening dress.*
    LINDA *gives a loud howl and hurriedly exits*)

BOBBY (*as he descends*) What's the matter with her? (*To John*) Is Gwen back?

STELLA. She'll be here in a few minutes.

BOBBY (*as he leaves the stairs*) Good. (*Smilingly*) I thought you'd had bad news.

JOHN. No—*we're* all right—but I don't know about *you*. (*Holding out the paper*) Have a look.

(BOBBY *crosses and takes the paper and moves away to* L *as* JOHN *continues*)

I'll get you a drink. You'll need it.

(JOHN *moves to the drinks table and pours a whisky.* BOBBY *looks up from the paper*)

BOBBY (*quietly*) It looks as though I've had it.

(STELLA *moves down, past the* R *end of the settee, to the* L *end front of the settee, as she says*)

STELLA (*over-cheerfully, to Bobby*) I don't think it'll do you much harm. After all, it's wonderful publicity, and everyone knows they use glycerine for tears on the films.

(BOBBY *sits in the armchair* LC *as* JOHN *moves towards him with the whisky, and says*)

JOHN (*irritably, to Stella*) It's not the same thing at all. Bobby earns his living making people cry. When they read about this, they'll laugh. (*To Bobby*) Did you really use an onion?
BOBBY. Yes.
JOHN (*holding it out*) Have a drink.
BOBBY (*with something of a smile*) No, thanks.
MICHAEL (*off; loudly*) Gwen, for heaven's sake, take it easy!
GWEN (*off; loudly*) I won't be bullied! I haven't done anything wrong!
JOHN. Ah! Here she is!
STELLA. Now, John, be tactful!
JOHN. I know how to deal with her!

(GWEN *enters through the archway, followed by* MICHAEL. *There is an air of defiance about her. She is wearing an old overcoat thrown over her evening dress and is carrying her shoes.* JOHN *continues*)

And about time too! Now listen to me, Gwen . . .
GWEN (*moving* C; *to John, coldly*) Are you still drinking?

(MICHAEL *moves up* RC)

JOHN (*angrily*) No, damn it, I am not! (*Placing the glass on the piano*) I poured it out for Denver!
STELLA (*moving to* R *of Gwen*) Shall I take your shoes? (*She takes them and looks at them*) My, my, you won't want these again, will you? Where did you get the overcoat?
MICHAEL (*moving from up* RC *to take the overcoat from Gwen's shoulders*) It belongs to an old boy who runs a coffee stall in Hammersmith.

(MICHAEL *throws the overcoat on to the back of the settee and moves to the* R *end of the settee*)

JOHN. Hammersmith? What the devil . . .?
STELLA (*interrupting, to Gwen*) Let's fix a nice hot bath, shall we?

(GWEN *nods—then looks at Michael, as she says, quietly*)

GWEN. Thank you for looking after me.
MICHAEL (*briskly*) Keep the old chin up. I'll be seeing you.
STELLA (*to Gwen*) Come on, honey.

(STELLA *puts her arm round* GWEN *and they move a step towards the stairs.* GWEN *stops suddenly and moves to* BOBBY)

GWEN (*quietly*) Have you read the papers?
BOBBY. One of them.
GWEN (*fighting back tears*) I'd give my life—not to have done that.
BOBBY (*rising*) Aw, skip it, Gwen. It's not going to knock me out. I'll be happier making people laugh.
GWEN (*breaking down*) I didn't *mean* to do it, Bobby! I didn't mean to!

(*Breaking down completely,* GWEN *turns and moves to* STELLA, *who puts an arm round her shoulders, as they ascend the stairs together, with* STELLA *saying*)

STELLA. Old Mr Skeffington's been looking for you. I found him on your bed this morning. I bet he gives you a lovely welcome.

(STELLA *and* GWEN *exit.* JOHN *immediately swallows the whisky, bangs down the glass, takes out his handkerchief and moves up* C, *as he blows his nose*)

MICHAEL (*to Bobby*) I know what you're thinking, but I didn't.
BOBBY. Didn't what?
MICHAEL. Give it to the papers. They collect those bits of news automatically.
BOBBY. That's all right.
JOHN (*to Michael*) Will there be any trouble about that river business?
MICHAEL (*smiling*) No, sir. You may have some chap call round, just to check up, but there's no question of attempted suicide. It was only a four-foot drop from the Embankment, and the tide was out. (*Having glanced at his watch*) Well, I'd better get to the office. (*He moves up* R) Cheeri-ho, Bobby.
BOBBY. So long, Michael.
JOHN. Shall we be seeing you again?
MICHAEL. I'm afraid so, sir. Gwen's going to write a novel and she wants me to help her with it.
JOHN. What about your job?
MICHAEL (*laughing out loud*) I've had that! Bobby was my assignment, and with me not cashing in on the onion they'll probably put me on to reporting stocks and shares or something.
JOHN (*enthusiastically*) Stocks and shares? Oh, my dear fellow! Come round as often as you like. Make this your home!
MICHAEL. Thank you, sir. That's the first time I've been invited back anywhere!

(*Laughing out loud,* Michael *exits through the archway*)

John (*to Bobby*) Nice fellow. Plenty of guts, too. So have you. *I* seem to be the only one without any.

(*Unseen by* John, Stella *enters to descend the stairs, as he continues*)

The youngest child is always the favourite, and mine hates me.

Stella (*from the stairs*) She'll love you again when she hears the truth about Pearl.

John (*having turned to Stella*) Well, why not tell her now?

(John *moves to join* Stella *on the stairs but, as he reaches the foot of them, the phone rings. He grabs the receiver*)

(*At the phone*) Hullo? . . . Hold on. (*To Bobby*) It's for you. Somebody called Charlie.

Bobby (*making for the phone*) Oh, Lord, that's my agent. This is going to be tricky. (*Having taken the receiver from John*) Hullo, Alfred . . . Yes, I've seen it . . . It's true . . . (*Suddenly and excitedly*) Are you fooling? . . . Sure! I'll be right round! (*He slams back the receiver. Excitedly, to John and Stella*) I've had an offer to play America! All cards on the table—and billed as "The Crooner who kidded London." (*He grabs his hat and overcoat, as he continues excited at the top of his voice—Al Jolson style*) California, here ah come!

Stella (*as with* John *she moves from upstairs*) When are you going?

Bobby. Right now!

John. Oh, my dear fellow, I'm so sorry. (*Happily, as he hurries to the archway*) I'll get you a taxi.

Stella (*moving to him*) Good-bye, Bobby.

Bobby (*giving her a peck on the cheek*) Good-bye, darling.

John (*impatiently waiting in the archway; to Bobby*) Get a move on!

Stella (*to Bobby*) Come and see us as soon as you get back.

Bobby. You bet!

Stella. Don't forget!

Bobby (*singing*)
>   I won't forget to remember,
>   Darling mine—

(*He turns and moves to the archway, as he continues*)

(*Singing*) Dearest, I didn't know—

(*In the archway, he is* L *of John, and he turns to Stella, as he continues*)

(*Singing*) How quickly those few hours would go—

John (*as he gives Bobby a jab in the behind with his knee*) Oh, get out!

(*Responding to the jab*, Bobby *makes an undignified exit—followed by* John—*but he continues to sing off stage*)

Bobby (*his singing fading to the distance, off*)
Since first I kissed your lips so red . . .

(Stella *looks a little sad. Then, she looks at the piano, sees the microphone still in position near the keyboard, and smiles. She moves to the microphone and switches it on. She sits at the piano—and plays and sings quickly "Cry".*

After the first two lines, John *comes hurrying back through the archway*)

John (*loudly*) Stella!

(*She stops*)

(*Continuing desperately*) I've reached the end of my tether! (*Emphatically*) *One more straw* on the back of my camel—and the slender thread of my sanity will snap!

(*Very excited,* Linda *comes galloping in through the archway to the* r *end of the settee as she gasps*)

Linda. Oh, sir—ma'am! Miss Corinne's arrived—with her husband!

(John *slaps a hand to his forehead, and staggers to collapse on the settee, as he shouts*)

John. Oh, no!

(Stella *has risen from the piano—and she moves to* lc *as* Corinne *comes hurrying in through the archway. She is dressed in modified cowgirl outfit, with modified Stetson*)

Corinne (*excitedly, as she immediately moves to embrace Stella*) Seventeen hours ago, we were in New York! Barnaby's sold that darned horse and we're staying right here just as long as we can!

(John *gives a loud moan and* Corinne *swings* Stella *round with her embrace as* Barnaby, *over six feet of dude cowboy, with ten-gallon Stetson and all the trappings, comes striding in through the archway. He makes straight for* Stella—*who has her back to him—swings her round, and lifts her high in the air, as he bellows*)

Barnaby (*lifting and lowering*) Hi-ya, Mom!

(John *reacts and goes all to pieces and, as* Barnaby *moves to him to grab a hand and shake the daylights out of him,* John *is gibbering, cross-eyed, twitching and shaking as* Barnaby *bellows*)

Mr Bentley, sir—you sure ain jerst as ah pictured yew!

Curtain

FURNITURE AND PROPERTY PLOT

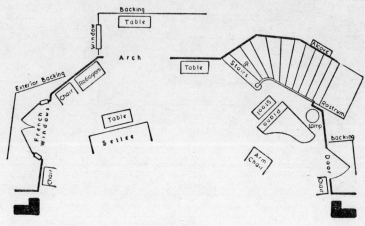

ACT I

On stage—Settee. *On it:* cushion
        Table (RC). *On it:* ashtray
        3 chairs
        Armchair
        Piano. *On it:* cigarette box
        Piano stool
        Table (R)
        Table (up C). *On it:* tray of drinks, whisky, gin, glasses, etc., telephone
        Radiogram
        In hall: table

Off stage—Mr Skeffington (LINDA)
        Airline valise (PAT)
        Plate with sandwich (LINDA)
        Bunch of yellow roses (STELLA)
        Copy of *Financial Times* (JOHN)
        Pat's coat (LINDA)
        Bunch of tulips, microphone with lead (BOBBY)

Personal—PAT: packet of French cigarettes, matches
        STELLA: handbag with press cutting, handkerchief
        BOBBY: braces, watch

French windows shut
Curtains open

ACT II

SCENE I

Set—*On settee:* black homburg.

Strike—Dirty glasses, etc.

Off stage—Tray with glass of milk (LINDA)
        2 medicine bottles wrapped (JOHN)
        Book (PAT)
        Suitcase (JOHN)

Personal—Bobby: torn hat, stocking
    John: handkerchief
    Pat: dark glasses
    Schneider: handkerchief
French windows open
Curtains open

SCENE 2

Strike—Suitcase

Off stage—Newspaper (Michael)
    Suitcase, parcel (Peter)

Personal—Peter: pipe, tobacco, matches
    Bobby: watch

French windows closed
Curtains open

ACT III

SCENE 1

Set—"Waiter." *On it:* 2 champagne bottles, empty glass
  On piano: glasses
  On table behind settee: 2 champagne bottles, brandy bottle half full, glasses
  On drinks table: Peter's parcel containing plasticine mould
  Move armchair close to piano
  Move small chair to R of the "waiter"

Off stage—Tray with coffee-pot, milk jug, 4 each cups, saucers, plates, knives,
    2 plates with sandwiches (Linda)

Personal—Peter: knitting and needles
    Schneider: cigar
    Bobby: onion, handkerchief

French windows shut
Curtains half drawn

SCENE 2

Strike—All empty bottles, glasses, etc.

Set—Chair by drinks table. *On it:* Bobby's overcoat and hat
  On settee: blanket

Off stage—Cup of tea (Linda)
    Newspaper (Linda)

Personal—Michael: watch

French windows closed
Curtains open

SONGS

Please Don't Forget to Remember.
  Campbell, Connelly & Co. Ltd, 10 Denmark Street, London, W.C.2

Sweet and Lovely.
  Keith Prowse & Co. Ltd, 42–43 Poland Street, London, W.1.

High Noon
Down Yonder
Cry

  Francis, Day & Hunter Ltd, 138–140 Charing Cross Road, London, W.C.2

LIGHTING PLOT

Property fittings required: Wall brackets

                                   Standard lamp

ACT I

A lounge
Interior. Morning
THE MAIN ACTING AREAS are round the settee (RC), by the archway
(up R), on the stairs (up L), round the piano (L), and round the arm-
chair (LC)
THE APPARENT SOURCE OF LIGHT is from the french windows (R)
OFF STAGE LIGHTING: Sunlight on window backing; strips or floods out-
side arch and stairs

To open: Bright; full stage lighting; sunlight through window
No cues

ACT II SCENE 1

To open: The same as for Act I except that shaft of sunlight should be slightly
altered
No cues

ACT II SCENE 2

THE APPARENT SOURCE OF LIGHT is from the practical lamps
OFF STAGE LIGHTING: Dusk outside french windows; strips or flood outside
stairs and arch

To open: Bright; practicals on
No cues

ACT III SCENE 1

OFF STAGE LIGHTING: Night sky outside french windows; strips or flood
outside arch and stairs

To open: bright; practicals on
No cues

ACT III SCENE 2

As for Act I
No cues

Any character costumes or wigs needed in the performance of this
play can be hired from Charles H. Fox Ltd, 25 Shelton Street, London,
WC2H 9HX